SIEGE AT JADOTVILLE

THE IRISH ARMY'S FORGOTTEN BATTLE

SIEGE AT JADOTVILLE

THE IRISH ARMY'S FORGOTTEN BATTLE

DECLAN POWER

BLACKSTONE
PUBLISHING

Copyright © 2011 by Declan Power
Published in 2016 by Blackstone Publishing
Cover art courtesy of Netflix
Book design by Kathryn Galloway English

First edition: 2016
ISBN 978-1-5047-5872-7

2 3 4 5 6 7 8 9 10

CIP data for this book is available
from the Library of Congress

Blackstone Publishing
31 Mistletoe Rd.
Ashland, OR 97520

www.BlackstonePublishing.com

To my parents, Maura and Anthony Power,
for their patience and guidance

FOREWORD

Many of you who purchase this book may have done so after watching the film adaption, and so may not be aware of the journey that has taken place to bring this story to a wider audience.

As I write this new foreword, it is almost fifty-five years since the men of A Company, 35ᵗʰ Irish Infantry Battalion of the UN force in the Congo, found themselves in a fight for their lives.

Little did those men, who were led by Commandant Pat Quinlan, realize the battle to restore their honor would take far longer and be a more uphill struggle.

Finally this struggle now appears to be at an end. The film provides the essence and heart of the story produced in this book. It is also the first time that Irish soldiers will feature in a major motion film.

If it does nothing else, it reminds us that there is a cost to helping keep peace and maintain stability and security. It is also a reminder to others that Ireland is not a passive state and that we honor our commitments to those less fortunate than ourselves.

I first met Richie Smyth, who directed the film adaption of this book, in October 2009. I had just stepped off a plane back from Darfur in Sudan, my head spinning from dealing with real life drama involving evacuations and kidnappings whilst working with the United Nations (UN). As Richie outlined his idea to turn the Jadotville story into film I thought I was hearing things and didn't believe it would happen.

But happen it did. And Richie stayed true to his promise that while he would be producing a film to thrill and entertain, he would not deviate from the accuracy of the core of the story. Not alone did he deliver on his word, he did so with verve, style, and artistry of a high order. I thank him for it.

It is now over eleven years since this book was first published in Ireland. Little did I then realize the trajectory it would take.

The book was launched by Willie O'Dea, a former Minister for Defence in Ireland. O'Dea is well known in Ireland as an astute politician and clever operator. When the request for him to launch the book was submitted, he insisted the book be studied by senior members of the department as well as at least one senior officer from the Irish Defence Forces, also known as Oglaigh na hEireann.

The response from those quarters resulted in him agreeing to launch the book, but also publicly honor the men of A Company through a commemorative plaque.

For some of the Jadotville veterans present that day, this was a significant victory in their struggle for official recognition of their bravery and restoration of their rightful military reputation.

O'Dea also addressed the Irish parliament, and made public statements exonerating and exhorting the actions of the men who fought at Jadotville whilst putting on the public record that Commandant Quinlan and his men had acquitted themselves of a high order in terms of military professionalism and valor.

But the saga did not stop there. Along with the commemorative plaque that was mounted in Custume Barracks in County Westmeath, a scroll was produced for each member of A Company by the Department of Defence and signed by O'Dea to attest to their professionalism.

However, for many veterans and campaigners, among them John Gorman and Leo Quinlan (the son of Pat Quinlan), there was still the issue of the military decorations that Quinlan himself had recommended for his men. Those who've seen the film will know that there was a less than positive response from the Irish state on this matter.

With the resultant attention from the film's creation and the republication of the book, both John Gorman and Leo Quinlan stepped up their agitation for recognition for the awards to be honored. It was extremely difficult to overturn a decision reached by a medals board convened by the Irish military in the 1960s. But nevertheless, the campaigners who were assisted by the Irish politician Kevin "Boxer" Moran, succeeded in their objective and military history was created.

As I write this, the Department of Defence and the Irish Defence Forces are in the process of creating a Unit Citation for the men of A Company.

This is a new award in the hierarchy of Irish military valor awards. It will mean for the first time a unit of the Irish Defence Forces can be decorated collectively for valor and professionalism in performing above and beyond the standard expected in a time of crisis and/or in a combat situation.

It will be a fitting legacy from the men who fought at Jadotville that a military honour will now exist for future units of the Irish Defence Forces to be decorated collectively for valor in action.

The words of the citation are still being worked on, but I was kindly allowed to see the proposed words which I can share with you now:

The Government of Ireland recognizes the leadership, courage, bravery, and professional performance of A Company, 35th Infantry Battalion, ONU and its Irish and Swedish attachments who, under changing circumstances at Jadotville while besieged by overwhelming numbers of Katanganese gendarmerie and cut off from support and reinforcements, did valiantly defend their position from 13 September 1961 to 17 September 1961.

A ceremony will take place to present the citation to the survivors of A Company and the next-of-kin of those men deceased. In time, the necessary arrangements will be made to amend Defence Force Regulations to create this as an official military decoration with accompanying insignia such as exists for our uniformed comrades in our sister nations of the United States of America and Australia.

As is mentioned in the acknowledgements section of this book, both now and previous, the Jadotville veteran John Gorman played a crucial role in this campaign. He kept pushing the door and the door kept opening further, bit by bit.

It was an irony not lost on many with military connections that one former corporal in the regular army (Gorman) and a former corporal in the reserves (O'Dea) were to be key figures in finally setting the record straight on the Jadotville affair.

Following a conversation with Gorman, O'Dea agreed the nature of the plaque to be created and installed at Custume Barracks commemorating the troops who fought at Jadotville and marking their place in Irish military history and being a reminder of the standard of professionalism required in the field to generations of other Irish soldiers.

Gorman, of course took it further, and on his own initiative, raised money to have the names of each man who served at Jadotville engraved on the plaque.

Gorman had been a long and lonely ball carrier on behalf of the Jadotville team for a long time. He never stopped running for the line no matter how many times he was brought to ground.

As his wife, Joan, and daughter, Sarah, know, those times were many, but he never stayed down for long. As he said once in response to an official who warned him to cease his agitation, "Gorman will continue to soldier on." And long may he do so.

There are others that are due honorable mention too. Commandant

W. G. (Liam) Donnelly, who had served as a captain and support platoon commander at Jadotville, had also done some time in this vineyard of hardship.

Donnelly produced a submission to the office of the Chief of Staff of the Irish Defence Forces in 1996. It is an erudite and concise analysis of the facts and circumstances surrounding events that led to the siege and subsequent events thereafter.

It's highly unusual for a retired officer to submit such a document to the Chief of Staff, however, as he stated himself in his introduction,

> The commander of a support platoon would normally be expected not to be overly concerned about the procedures and orders from a higher authority, only to obey them when lawful. However, in the circumstances in which A Company found itself at Jadotville and the manner in which the Jadotville affair was glossed over… led me to gather information to assist in…clearing the good name, professional integrity, and bravery of all the A Company personnel in relation to the Jadotville affair.

There is no need for me to quote much further, as much of Donnelly's submission forms the spine of much of my book. His material was considered so controversial in some military quarters that it was passed to me by some on condition that its origin not be revealed. I have honoured that request, until now.

Donnelly's research and information was left to languish in a dusty file in the headquarters of the Irish Defence Forces for too long. He himself later confided to me at a Jadotville veteran's event that he felt it had gone no-where and he had put too much faith in the military system in trying to get matters resolved.

As I write this I wish to record that without the information gathered by him and transmitted to me by others, this book would not have been the success it became, and indeed it is unlikely the film would have been made.

In as much as Gorman took on and fought the political and military establishments and won, Donnelly's work formed the basis for success on a broader canvas. His family, his colleagues, and the soldiers of the Irish Defence Forces should be proud of him and thankful to him. I am personally grateful to him for his scholarship.

Another honorable mention must go to Walter Hegarty, the recipient of a Distingushed Services Medal (DSM). Now, like many of the surviving veterans of Jadotville and in common with Donnelly, Hegarty fights a determined battle against serious illness.

I know his family and friends consider him a hero and he certainly defines the meaning of the term. He led from the front and was loyal to all and throughout all ordeals, including his current one, he displays good humor and sparkling wit. He epitomizes the spirit of the Irish soldier, past, present, and future, and I for one am proud to have worn the same uniform as him.

Noel Carey was fearful when I first approached him about contributing to this book. But it was my good fortune that I won over his concerns and he granted me access to his notes, diary, and reports.

His insights and candid accounts of his personal feelings during the time of the siege were of immense value. Carey has gone on to share these insights of the experience of battle with a number of generations of young officers of the Irish Defence Forces.

Thankfully the Irish military college are aware of the benefits of such insights for leadership development within our forces and the need to hear from veterans on the moral impact of decisions in the field.

Carey continues to lecture on Jadotville and to be of assistance to his former colleagues in whatever way he can. In common with all of his surviving comrades, he is a stalwart steward of the spirit of Jadotville.

There are other men who were not serving in Irish uniform who did their bit at Jadotville. The interpreter, Lt. Lars Fromberg, and the helicopter pilots, Bjarne Hovden and Eric Thors, have all been mentioned in the book and listed with the nominal roll at the end.

But there were some others worthy of mention. Charles Kearney, an Irish national, and Hamish Mathieson, a Scotsman, who were both working as mining engineers in Jadotville when A Company came under attack, assisted A Company by passing vitally important tactical information to Commandant Quinlan.

The two civilians were later captured when accompanying a UN reconnaissance team under the command of Captain Mick Purfield, who was later to be awarded a DSM for risking his life to go behind enemy lines and negotiate for the lives of Irish prisoners threatened with execution.

While Charles Kearney is now deceased and the whereabouts of his valiant Scottish colleague is unknown, Kearney's wife Julie is still with us and now resides in County Wexford.

It would not be too much to ask that the state make gesture of recognition to the widow and existing family of Kearney for his patriotism.

Finally, it is my belief that other players in this drama, such as the then 35th Infantry Battalion commander, Lt. Col. Hugh McNamee, and Commandant Johnny Kane, the commanding officer of the rescue force at Lufira Bridge, all acted honorably during difficult and challenging times.

I also extend a note of thanks and recognition to those others who raised this issue in an attempt to see a wrong righted. Rose Doyle's book *Heroes of Jadotville* and Mick Whelan's book *Battle of Jadotville* were published in the years following the initial publication of this book. They made honorable contributions to raising awareness of the matter.

I feel the record has been set straight on the siege at Jadotville. Let those of us now associated with this in the Irish defense community close ranks and *agus ar aghaidh leat* (move forward)!

Declan Power
August 2016
Dublin

1

SIEGE AT JADOTVILLE

Those that I fight I do not hate,
Those that I guard I do not love.

—WILLIAM BUTLER YEATS,
"AN IRISH AIRMAN FORESEES HIS DEATH"

The cry went up, *"Le majeur irlandais!"* and the crowd surged forward, straining to grasp the hand of the Irish officer as he attempted to enter the small bar in Jadotville town.

As the officer entered the bar, a command rang out and the assembled mercenaries snapped to attention. Commandant Pat Quinlan (forty-two), the commanding officer of A Company, part of the 35th Irish Battalion of the UN forces, must have found the scene quite ironic. These respectful men, braced with their stomachs in and chests out, had been locked in mortal combat with Quinlan's men only twenty-four hours previously.

Both sides were now applying a cease-fire and Quinlan had gone into town to buy some beer for his troops who were parched. No other liquid was available.

C'est la guerre, Quinlan mused to himself, if indeed "war" was the correct term that could be applied to the bizarre conflict that he and his men had been sucked into.

Here he was, buying beer in a bar filled with men who had been trying to kill him and his troops only twenty-four hours beforehand. A lean man with a soldierly frame, Quinlan steadily elbowed his way toward the bar.

With his mouth firmly clenched and his eyes unblinking under his shaggy brows, he returned the gaze of each and every mercenary who tried to stare him down.

Following closely behind him was Warrant Officer Eric Thors, a Swedish helicopter pilot, who had assisted in flying the ill-fated and only attempt the UN made to resupply Quinlan's besieged troops.

Despite the praise being lavished upon him, Quinlan was acutely aware that it was his troops who had accounted for the deaths of many messmates of the mercenaries ranged around him.

Some of the mercs, as the Irish soldiers called them, even came forward proudly to show off the wounds they had acquired. Quinlan nodded his appreciation, no doubt noting with satisfaction the marksmanship of his previously unbloodied teenage troops. Being a Kerryman, Quinlan was now demonstrating that mix of stoicism and sharpness his countymen are famed for. The local police guards were keen for Quinlan to leave before the mercs began to feel maudlin about their fallen comrades.

But Quinlan was damned if he was going back to his lads empty-handed. He'd promised them beer and beer they'd get. It wasn't just as a reward for holding their ground in the face of overwhelming odds. The plain truth of it was that the water had been cut off, and what had been saved was beyond stagnant in the harsh African heat. A crate of minerals had been delivered after the cease-fire, but it was no substitute for turning the water back on so his men could wash and slake their thirst. After all, they had been fighting in slit trenches for the last week. Following four days of intense combat that had included being strafed by a jet, Quinlan and his men were still in their positions when the Katangan gendarmes sought a cease-fire.

"We fought them to a standstill. If only the bloody relief column could have made it across Lufira Bridge, we'd be drinking those beers back in Elisabethville," Quinlan thought.

With his blue UN beret clamped on his head, and armed only with the natural authority of the career officer, Quinlan saw the assembled ranks of mercs part as he finally got to the bar and ordered his beer. As he was leaving the bar with his police escort a voice enquired, "*Mon commandant*, 'ow many men 'ave you lost?" Quinlan drew his hand across his moustache and eyed the French merc. "None," he replied, and strode smartly into the night.

"*Non! C'est incroyable! Ce n'est pas possible!*" the mercs mumbled among themselves. After all, hadn't they thrown everything they had against these peasant Irish? Hadn't they been strafing them with a jet each day of the campaign? Hadn't the pilot radioed them to tell them of the lineup of bodies behind the trenches covered in sheets?

More to the point, hadn't they themselves lost over 300 men? Le majeur irlandais, he was mad, or bluffing ... or both! In fact, Quinlan was neither. His journey into Jadotville had been quite calculated. Having had to fight with the absolute minimum number needed for such a defensive operation, and having received only one attempt at resupply, Quinlan was aware his men were starving and exhausted. As he recorded in his own account of the battle (which had been previously classified):

Many of the men have lost considerable weight and suffered from lack of sleep. Our only food now was some biscuits, and we had absolutely no water whatever. At approx. 1400 hours [I] insisted on going to Jadotville town on the pretext of buying some beer for the men. My real reason was to get the feel and attitude of the people. I asked two policemen to accompany me and I took Warrant Officer Eric Thors (Swedish copilot of the helicopter) as interpreter. I drove through the town. It was armed with several hundred Gendermarie [sic] and armed civilians on the streets. One group of civilians jeered us. The police showed me a bar where I could get beer. I pulled the car in and when I got out a murmur went through the crowd.

It is apparent that even though he was the senior officer of the Irish contingent fighting at Jadotville, Quinlan was keenly aware that he lacked the knowledge he needed to make informed decisions about his plight.

However, he still had his tactical wits about him and, although he had acceded to a cease-fire at the request of the opposing forces, Quinlan knew that his company was in a tactically perilous situation. Deployed to the Congo with the 35th Battalion of the United Nations Operation in the Congo (ONUC) to keep the peace and enforce UN resolutions, Quinlan and his men found themselves fighting a classic company-in-defense action without the necessary weapons and tools to carry out such a task.

The Irish troops were attending Mass parade behind their positions when Katangan soldiers with their European mercenary officers launched a sneak attack on the morning of September 13, 1961. They were repulsed thanks to the quick actions of a small number of troops pulling sentry duty and the swift reaction of the troops from Mass parade. The men of A Company, though youthful and largely inexperienced, pulled well together when battle was joined at Jadotville. Despite the majority of the company being at Mass, a number of sentries had been posted along the Irish positions.

At 0735 hours, the enemy jeeps, equipped with mounted machine guns and clustered with troops, sped towards the Irish positions. The Katangans were relaxed and in jocular cowboy mode, sprawled across their vehicles and toting their automatic weapons.

And why wouldn't they be happy and feel confident? Hadn't their officers told them of les irlandais and their constant need for speaking to their God? Wasn't their fear of the Black Warrior such that les irlandais were having ceremonies with their ju-ju man every morning?

The poor fools wouldn't even be manning any defensive positions. It would be a rout, like shooting fish in a barrel.

Indeed, the Irish were at Mass parade that morning, as they were most mornings, and this information on their movements had been communicated to the mercenary officers. Members of the white civilian community around Jadotville were to play more than a bystander's role in the battle that unfolded. Sometimes this was to the benefit of the Irish, but, as the September morn unfolded, this civilian input directly led to conflict. For it was a Belgian settler who had tipped off the Katangan forces about the Irish routine, and had advised an attack when they were at their weakest.

The fact that it was a Mass parade also gave the mercenary officers a psychological weapon with which to motivate their native troops and give them confidence of a quick, easy fight against a less confident adversary. The psychological element was to play a leading part in both the tactical and strategic nature of operations in Katanga.

The Katangans now rushed forward, firing short bursts from their jeeps in the hopes of killing or spooking whichever Irishmen spotted them first.

However, their hopes of a quick kill were dashed by a bit of Offaly flair and élan. Showing the same self-possession and calmness in adversity as his countymen have often done on All-Ireland final days, Sgt. John Monaghan met the Katangans head-on with a burst of the finest Vickers machine-gun lead.

Monaghan was returning to his trench after shaving when he

spotted the swiftly approaching vehicles. Realizing an attack was under way, and with a minimum of time to do all that must have rushed through his head, Monaghan acted in the finest tradition of NCO leadership.

Unlike the senior leadership on many UN operations, or indeed the UN Security Council, Monaghan didn't mull over this dilemma for long. After all, he was a professional soldier, not a politician or diplomat. Shouting a warning to the few subordinate soldiers, mostly young, unseasoned midlands lads, still in his vest with his shaving towel draped around his shoulders, he vaulted across a nearby trench to get to his destination.

"The Vickers! I've got to get to the Vickers! If they keep coming I'll need its firepower to pin them down until the rest of the lads make it back from the Mass parade."

The Vickers was a water-cooled belt-fed machine gun that had been used to devastating effect by the British Army in the many theaters of WWII. It was one of the few support-type weapon assets that A Company had at its disposal during the battle. The few available Vickers machine guns were sited to cover any route of strategic advance on the Irish positions.

By making the decision to man the gun and warn the few sentries, Monaghan certainly gave his fellow soldiers time to react and get to their positions. He also gave his superiors time to adapt their plans of defense to the rapidly unfolding drama that was developing that sunny September morning.

For most, the mere fact that heavily armed forces were advancing rapidly on their positions would have constituted a hostile act. But showing true presence of mind and a sense of mission, Monaghan did not open fire until the Katangans had fired the first shots.

John Gorman, now a retired veteran noncommissioned officer (NCO), then a seventeen-year-old private in his first year of service, remembers the initial deployment to Jadotville:

We were always drilled about not commencing hostilities first. We were there as UN, to keep the peace and to avoid causing conflict. "Don't be the first to fire," we were always told. Sure isn't that how the Balubas killed the lads at Niemba? We sacrificed men to the notion of not being first to fire. But John Monaghan got the balance right. He had his machine gun cocked and ready, and at the first burst he let them have it.

But he fired over their heads.

"He gave them a chance to retreat. Once they weren't a threat, why kill them directly and increase tension?" remembers Gorman.

But it didn't really matter, tactically. The main thing was that Monaghan had broken the thrust of the Katangans' attack. The jeeps were now swaying wildly and the once-cocky troops had cleansed their faces of mirth.

Les irlandais weren't all at Mass. Some of these damned Irish were actually firing back. Not just any shots either, but an accurate and disciplined burst of machine-gun fire. The mercenary officers appeared shocked to see them respond.

As the other Irish troops, rushing into their positions, commenced returning small-arms fire, the main body of the battalion had been alerted. Some of the troops attending Mass parade had brought their personal weapons with them and were quickly able to run back to their positions and return fire.

One of these was twenty-nine-year-old Sgt. Walter Hegarty, the platoon sergeant of No. 2 Platoon of A Company. He had been at the Mass parade and had insisted on taking his Swedish submachine gun with him. Known as the Gustaf, it was magazine fed and fired nine mm pistol-caliber ammunition over short distances.

In this account he recalls how his spiritual reverie was interrupted by flying lead:

Wednesday saw us up and about as normal. Down the road to No. 1 Platoon lines for Mass went a bunch of us. The only one with his Gustaf was yours truly and so had to endure much chaffing. But in ten minutes I was a happy man when the gends (an abbreviation Irish troops used for the Katangan gendarmerie, the force ranged against them) hove into sight and commenced firing.

Time—0740, and Mass had been just a few minutes in progress. After spasmodic firing on both sides, things quieted down. We had breakfast in the trenches and the chaplain began his rounds giving general absolution on tick. [Fr.] Fagan, who is normally stationed at Gormanstown [a small camp and former airfield outside of Dublin], is a true priest.

One of the platoon commanders, Lt. Noel Carey (twenty-four), a Limerick native, was driving out to A Company's outer positions when the attack began:

As I arrived, I observed Katangan troops dismounting from trucks across the road from Support Platoon. I roared at the lads to occupy the trenches and moved on to No. 1 Platoon area as many of them were gathering for outdoor Mass. I alerted them to get into cover and then proceeded towards Purfina Garage, our Company HQ.

As I was driving along the road, the first burst of gunfire rang out, and it was a dreadful feeling not knowing if this fire was aimed at me and the jeep.

The fire that the young officer heard at that point was undoubtedly Sgt. Monaghan engaging the Katangan raiding party with the belt-fed WWII-vintage Vickers machine gun.

That the Irish were attending a Mass parade, rather than in their trenches prepared for attack, could initially be construed as soldierly naïveté on their part. But as this story unfolds, we shall see just what an impossible and confused situation the men of Comdt. Quinlan's A Company had been faced with in trying to attain their objectives at Jadotville. To begin with, the very objectives they were furnished with seemed vague and at times downright contradictory.

However, one thing is certainly clear. Before deployment to Jadotville, neither Comdt. Quinlan nor anyone else in the UN authority in the Congo was expecting A Company to end up in a pitched battle with well-armed and well-led troops.

As John Gorman recalls:

We were given to believe that there were white European settlers there that had to be protected. We supposed that meant from the Baluba tribesmen. This meant dealing with a force that largely used bows and arrows and, while brave, did not have military training and discipline.

Before we arrived, our sister unit, B Company, had been based there, as had a Swedish company. But both had been moved before we were sent in. We never did get an answer as to why two companies were moved out and then we were sent in.

One thing in particular stuck in my head from that time. I remember seeing posters being put up by the white settlers after we arrived, saying, "A Company—Go Home!" This struck me as a strange sort of a welcome from people we had been sent to protect. In fact, I didn't see anyone out to welcome us. It seemed to us that all the whites there were totally against us, against the UN.

Gorman's recollection is just one of many anomalies that crop up when one looks at the issues and reasons leading to the deployment of A Company to Jadotville.

One of the most glaring problems, however, was not to arise from Machiavellian political maneuvering, but from simple equipment problems.

The troops had been ordered in to secure a position without the necessary tools. An infantry unit should have a complement of what are termed "support weapons." These should include medium-range mortars, machine guns, and other weapons that give a suite of options to a commander trying to defend a position from sustained attack.

Added to this were further problems bedeviling A Company. Transport to Jadotville broke down and prevented the delivery of necessary equipment. Some of the radio sets were also faulty and only worked intermittently throughout the battle.

But then transport and communications were problems which were a source of irritation to the entire Irish contingent, having been deployed to carry out a complex and difficult job with largely vintage equipment.

It is interesting to note that although A Company was the third unit to occupy the ground around Jadotville, they were the first to dig fighting trenches in order to have a proper defensive formation. Walter Hegarty notes that the Irish troops' ability to break the attack was really only down to one thing: "The first thing Comdt. Quinlan had the company do when they arrived at J.Ville [*sic*] was dig in. B Company, whom we replaced, had no trenches."

In fact, many of the veterans attribute their survival to this order from Comdt. Quinlan. CQMS Pat Neville puts it succinctly: "Comdt. Quinlan's order to dig trenches undoubtedly saved lives and enabled us to put up a resistance."

However, within days of deployment to Jadotville, most of these issues became academic to the soldiers of A Company, as they found themselves in a real shooting war for the first time.

Most of the troops, regardless of age, had seen very little action before. The company had been involved in a long-range patrol and an operation involving weapon seizure from mercenary officers.

Neville, who is now retired but was then the CQMS for A Company, was one of the two senior noncommissioned officers in the unit and responsible for overseeing the supply and welfare of the troops:

> While the two previous actions were not big shooting matches, they gave the lads a chance to settle into their job. You must remember they were mostly very young, still in their teens many of them. While they were reasonably well trained, the previous operations helped them find their feet, but more importantly gave them the opportunity to develop trust in their leaders.

> It must be remembered that while some of the NCOs and officers were very experienced in leading men, none of us had any real experience of combat.

Certainly the mercenary officers were aware of the Irish troops' equipment shortcomings and their relative lack of experience in practicing the art of war on a real battlefield. Indeed, a European mercenary officer captured by A Company during the fighting testified to the diverse and wide experience of the mercenary forces ranged against them. All had been veterans of either WWII or France's colonial adventure in Vietnam. Indeed, many were veterans of both.

With the element of surprise and the lack of certain support weapons, it would not have been unexpected for a force like A Company to lose the initiative and panic, allowing their enemy to outmaneuver them in those crucial early elements of the battle.

Lt. Carey recalls A Company's response to the battle following their recovery from the surprise attack:

Suddenly, there was a cry from my forward trench that Katangan forces were observed coming across scrub ground immediately to our front. I rushed to the trench and after a few minutes with heart thumping, I clearly observed the Katangans, at about six hundred yards, coming through the scrub towards us.

Tom Quinlan's platoon (an officer later to be decorated with the DSM for actions undertaken at a later date during his Congo service) to my right began to engage, and in my anxiety I grabbed the Bren gun, as I could not engage with my Gustaf submachine gun at long range.

After getting direction from my driver, Private Boland, I began to engage the Katangans. There was absolutely no doubt in my mind we were under fire from an unprovoked attack and were fully justified in defending ourselves.

The Katangans retreated out of sight. At the same time I heard the crump of mortar fire directed at our comrades in No. 1 Platoon and Support Platoon's positions and could clearly hear the rattle of machine-gun fire. What was happening? How were our lads holding out? It was a dreadful feeling not knowing what was happening. Then the firing started to slacken and, apart from small-arms fire, the time passed and we felt we had repulsed their efforts.

These reminiscences by Lt. Carey give a hint of the adrenaline rush that was taking place in the bodies of these youthful soldiers encountering combat for the first time.

They also indicate one thing that all soldiers will recognize—the sheer confusion that begins to reign when battle is joined. Considering the youth of these troops and the fact that they were now outnumbered by the opposing Katangan forces, it is remarkable that the Katangans did not manage to break through in the first stages of battle.

However, the issue of the now much-needed support weapons came to the fore. These machine guns and mortars would have given the beleaguered A Company an ability to engage the enemy from a greater distance and so stop an enemy advance in its tracks before it threatened the Irish trench lines.

Though the opening attack had been broken, the initial euphoria experienced by the Irish troops was not long to be enjoyed.

Before the adrenaline rush had even subsided from this first taste of combat, large forces of the Katangan gendarmerie were observed moving into position on A Company's flanks.

A study carried out for a Command and Staff course at the Irish Defence Force Military College gently notes that Comdt. Quinlan did not take tactical advantage of this and what the consequences may have been:

> The Coy Commander (Quinlan) gave an order to hold fire at this stage in the hope of defusing the situation. In hindsight, this may have been a valuable target opportunity lost.

While certainly a valid comment regarding a unit commander's role in a combat situation—that is, to close with the enemy and destroy him by every means possible—it does not take into account the strategic and political waters Quinlan had to navigate. As we shall see in later chapters, Quinlan was effectively trying to sail his unit through waters with only a half-drawn map courtesy of UN strategic planning and communications, or rather the lack thereof.

One reason Quinlan may have hesitated before ordering his troops to cut down the advancing Katangans may have been the confusion surrounding larger scale UN operations such as Operation Morthor at Elisabethville.

This action had not yet finished, but radio communication to Quinlan declared that it had. Therefore, he naturally assumed his forces would be operating from a position of superiority.

In his after-action report he notes:

> There was a lull in fighting for approximately two and a half hours, but we observed large forces of the gendarmerie moving into positions on our flanks. We could have inflicted heavy casualties at this stage but I ordered [machine guns] and mortars to hold fire as the news from E'ville was good and there was a chance that the attack of the morning was the action of hotheads.

His mens' morale was also high as word had been sent that a relief column was on the way from Irish Battalion HQ at Elisabethville, which was now supposed to be totally secure in UN hands.

However, reality, psychology, and communications were to become weapons every bit as potent as the mortar shell or grenade in the action that was to follow.

Although he didn't know it then, Quinlan would have to wage this battle much like a prizefighter climbing into the ring blindfolded and with one arm tied behind his back.

However, his foresight was to save his men's lives. As well as ordering his men to dig trenches after they arrived, he ordered that all available receptacles be filled with fresh water, even though he was expecting reinforcements by the end of the day. These actions were to mean the difference between life and death.

Lt. Carey notes:

Through Company Sergeant Jack Prendergast, I got word that a relief column was on the way from our battalion at Elisabethville and would be at the Lufira bridge soon. Morale soared as I informed the platoon in the trenches adjacent to me. We had no food and only a little water, but the adrenaline kept all those thoughts out of our mind, even in the blistering heat.

We discussed how we would greet our relief column and how well we had acquitted ourselves after the baptism of fire. As the day passed, we could clearly hear the thump of mortars at Lufira and our hearts soared. Our relief was at hand. The firing lasted for just over an hour and then silence. We waited and waited.

While the younger men watched the proceedings over the battle sites of their new FN assault rifles, the arrogance of youth and the flush of seeing retreating Katangans earlier riddled any fear in their heart.

By 1130 hours, all that had changed. For the next four days, A Company would be embroiled in a battle that would become more and more desperate, but throughout which they would fight with the utmost bravery.

2

PRELUDE TO A FIGHT

They must to keep their certainty accuse
All that are different of a base intent;
Pull down established honor; hawk for news
Whatever their loose fantasy invent.

—WILLIAM BUTLER YEATS,
"THE LEADERS OF THE CROWD"

As events unfolded at Jadotville, there were times when individual soldiers wondered why they were fighting for their lives under a searing African sun far from home.

The events that led to A Company going to Africa go back to the untangling of the Congo from its colonial masters, the Belgians.

For a shrinking number of Irish people, the Congo will always be synonymous with the army and UN service. But Ireland's involvement in that ill-fated country was largely confined to a province called Katanga that had attempted to break away from the rest of the country.

The Congo is the third largest country on the African continent. It is to be found sitting on the equator and is surrounded by the Central African Republic and Sudan to the north, and Angola and Zambia to the south.

In its own right, the Congo is nearly the size of Western Europe, at approximately 900,000 square miles. The center and north of the country are covered with thick, tropical rain forest, while the south is mainly bush and tundra.

The whole country has a climate that is very hot and humid and quite energy sapping. European involvement in the Congo commenced with the advent of Portuguese settlers in 1483, but this was limited until King Leopold II of Belgium set up trading concessions there in 1879. Because of his financial investment, the country came to be regarded as the King's personal property.

The Belgian government officially took possession of the country in 1908, renaming it the Belgian Congo.

At the time, there were six provinces in the Congo: Équateur, Orientale to the north; Léopoldville, Kasaï, and Kivu to the south. To the southeast was Katanga, bordering the British-backed Federation of Rhodesia.

The country was administered from Brussels, with a governor general in each of the six provinces.

Becoming a Belgian colony did not change the way of life much for the native Congolese population. The Belgian regime focused on developing the Congo's economic value, expressly with a view to utilizing the region's expansive natural resources.

One of the spin-offs of colonization, however, was the development of a sophisticated communications network throughout the country.

By the 1950s, the Congo, already blessed with a useful river system that spanned the country, now had roads, railways, and airfields. The Belgians also installed telephone and radio services that were state of the art for Africa at that time.

Katanga was the jewel in the Belgian colonial crown. In 1960, as independence grew to be more than just an aspiration, Katanga was supplying 10 percent of the world's copper, 60 percent of its cobalt, and large quantities of diamonds.

These precious minerals not only meant that Katanga was a wealth-driving engine for the Congo, they also shunted the province into the arena of Cold War international strategy. Katanga produced nearly half the metals needed for the manufacture of jet engines and radar apparatuses in the western world.

As a result, quite a number of European and American companies had established major outlets in the province. Probably foremost among them was the Belgian company, Union Minière Du Haut Katanga, generally referred to as Union Minière. Union Minière functioned much as a small state within a state, being given carte blanche by the Belgians to go about its operations. With plenty of cheap native labor and no shortage of skilled European technicians, the company was one of the most successful in Africa.

Naturally this frantic commercial production led to considerable attention from the Soviet Union and their Eastern Bloc allies.

At the dawn of the swinging sixties, the Congo had found itself to be, quite fashionably, the center of attention for both parties of the Cold War. Both sides sought to increase their level of influence in the region.

In the midst of this economic siphoning and political jockeying for position, the Congolese people decided to commence their bid for independence.

As if this wasn't complicated enough, owing to Cold War machinations and Belgian desires to hold on to their colonial cash cow, the native population faced more prosaic obstacles.

Unlike other colonial masters, like the British, the Belgians never attempted to educate the native population in areas like civil administration or political structure. Higher education had become available to a select few after 1954 when it was decided it would benefit the colonial administration, but, for the vast majority of the native population, development of an indigenous political infrastructure was seen as irrelevant.

At this time there were two hundred tribes living in the Congo, mainly in rural regions. For most Congolese, membership of these tribes determined the type of lives they lived. The Belgian administrators rarely interfered in tribal affairs.

The most prolific of these tribes were the Baluba. They were accorded a certain respect by the other tribes: the Belgians also relied on them as the unskilled and semiskilled labor to operate the country's infrastructure.

However, they were not universally accepted throughout the Congo and particularly lacked influence in the capital, Léopoldville, and even in their own home province of Katanga.

Therefore, unlike other countries that agitated for independence, there was no single national identity within the native Congolese. The single bonding factor with those who advocated independence was a desire to see the back of the Belgians.

The Belgians had no intention of quitting Africa, but they could not ignore the reality of what British Prime Minister Harold Macmillan was to call "the wind of change" that was about to sweep across Africa. Both Britain and France, the most powerful colonial powers, were putting in place procedures for handing over their colonies to native governments.

Ghana, a former British colony, became independent in 1957, heralding the beginning of black Africa. In 1958, French Premier Charles de Gaulle offered French colonies full independence with membership within a French community of nations. As they relinquished power with one hand, the colonial powers were still keeping an influential foot-in-country.

Therefore, the Belgians knew they could not continue to rule as before. It would soon become impossible, as the Congolese started more and more to see their black African neighbors, at least titularly, holding the reins of power.

Out of necessity, as they did want to lose control of their interests in the region, the Belgians investigated avenues towards granting independence.

Previously, in 1955, the Institute for Colonial Studies in Antwerp had drafted a thirty-year plan to create the necessary systems and native leadership for a transition to independence.

But the increasing number of civil disturbances throughout the country were demonstrating the fact that such a lengthy period of transition was not acceptable to the native population. This resulted in the Belgians rapidly bringing forward their preparations for Congolese independence, without the level of planning that was required. Freedom of speech for the press and freedom of association were granted by charter in 1959.

Elections had also been held in 1957, but were restricted to local officials in the three biggest cities: Léopoldville (now called Kinshasa), Elisabethville, and Jadotville.

In 1959, after riots in Jadotville by the native population, the opportunity to vote was extended throughout the rest of the provinces. This was accompanied by a Belgian acceptance of the right of the native Congolese to independence.

In October 1959, the colonial authorities attempted to diffuse tension by proposing the creation of a central Congolese government with limited powers for 1960.

But for native activists, this was too little, too late.

In fact, it did nothing except create further tension, which led to the Brussels Round Table Conference.

Held in January of 1960, the conference attempted to foist a four-year transitional plan for independence on the Congolese delegates. This was rejected in no uncertain terms by the Congolese spokesman, Patrice Lumumba, a man who would later become the Congo's first prime minister.

Lumumba, a former postal clerk, was one of the few Congolese with the benefit of training in the public services and an understanding of how his colonial masters operated. He admired Belgian methods of governance, but hated being controlled by them.

As a rising leader within the Congolese independence movement, Lumumba was also courted by the Soviets. By 1960, he had become the meat in a Cold War sandwich. His attempts to create a new Congo in the face of such conflicting pressures was to lead to the implosion of his fledgling state.

Perhaps if he had moved a little bit more slowly, if there had been more patience to create the necessary glue to hold a national identity in place, the Congo might have taken its first steps into independence with a greater certainty.

Instead, Lumumba, yielding to the impatient mood of the Congolese people and the changes taking place throughout Africa, insisted on immediate independence.

The end result at the Brussels Conference was a tired Belgian acquiescence to the Congolese delegates' demand for autonomy. Keen to avoid being dragged into messy colonial wars like their European neighbors, the Belgians announced that on June 30, 1960, independence would be granted.

This meant a colony peopled with diverse tribes, having no national identity or native class trained for public administration, was to take control of its own affairs in less than five months. Not exactly a recipe to inspire confidence.

However, for the Belgians, this seemed the most suitable path to preserve their economic interests in the region. They still saw themselves and their administrative class playing a major role in the day-to-day running of Congolese affairs.

The simple fact was that all governance of the Congo was by Europeans. The native Congolese had no role in running the country, except at very low levels.

The overall idea was that this professional Belgian civil service class would remain after independence to run the country under a native political leadership. Gradually native administrators would be filtered into the system as they became more experienced.

Considering the fact that the Belgians had only started a system of progressing native Congolese into middle-management positions in 1957, this was going to require time and patience. Certainly, they did not realize what a problem this would be when they got their independence.

However, not all Congolese would be happy with such a carbon copy of Belgian administration. In a document entitled *The Manifesto* by Congolese political activist Joseph Iléo, who later became the Congo's prime minister, the author politely but firmly rejects any concept of the Congo becoming an African copy of Belgium. Iléo states:

> The present manifesto is only a point of departure. We will sharpen and complete it together with those who come later to join us…The next thirty years will be decisive for our future. It would be vain to base our national sentiment on attachment to the past. It is toward the future that we must turn our attention…We will only find this new equilibrium in the synthesis of our African character and temperament with the fundamental riches of Western civilization…We wish to be civilized Congolese, not dark-skinned Europeans.

The economic and commercial sectors were no better than the political and administrative arena. The new Belgian policy of a quick jump towards sovereignty was now to be sabotaged, largely by their own previous policies in the areas of education and progression.

Despite the Congo having one of the highest literacy levels throughout Africa—roughly between 40 and 60 percent of the population could read and write—no effort had been made to educate for leadership and responsibility.

While educational opportunities were broadly available at primary level throughout the Congo, these tended to shudder to a halt when children reached fourteen years of age, sometimes even before. Most education was provided through state-subsidized Roman Catholic schools. Fewer than 25,000 Congolese people had obtained any second-level education at the time, and only 30 had made it to university.

Notwithstanding the paucity of native candidates for middle and upper leadership positions, this native leadership vacuum was to prove fatal for the Congolese security forces.

Security in the Belgian Congo was provided by a paramilitary outfit called the Force Publique. By 1960, it stretched to a formidable 25,000 men who carried out the functions of both the army and police. Like all armies and most colonial police forces, it had a rigid rank structure. The commissioned officer corps numbered 1,100 and was entirely composed of white Europeans, mostly Belgian. The Force Publique's role in Congolese society was to enforce the colonial laws, keep order, protect property, and secure the border against threats. This they managed to do consistently and efficiently.

As an arm of colonial power, the Force had a number of things going for it. The lack of a cohesive national identity meant the native Congolese rank and file were loyal to the Force as opposed to any abstract idea of nation. For the ordinary Force Publique soldier, authority was enforced by his white officers. Whether there was a native government or not meant little. He would still receive his orders in the same way. The system of white officers doing the thinking and leading had already enabled the enlisted ranks of the

Force to be used effectively in punitive actions against their fellow countrymen.

The Force worked particularly well when the officer corps ensured members of different tribes were recruited for service outside their normal tribal boundaries. They exploited tribal loyalties in order to keep unit cohesion, which was a useful tool of colonial control. Being in the Force was just like being in a large tribe, as far as the enlisted ranks were concerned. At best, tribal rather than national identity was to prove one of the more significant problems for the new regime in the early days of independence, and at worst, the precursor to bloody mayhem. Moreover, the prevailing Belgian attitude to Congolese independence was relentlessly self-interested.

It was summed up in an article by M. Staelens in the journal *La Relève*. He wrote:

In fact, our [Belgian] policy reflected a background of…a rather Machiavellian calculation…He [De Schrijver, the responsible Belgian Minister] granted independence immediately, but without carrying out any of the reforms urged. The reason for this is that he never intended conferring on the Congolese anything more than a purely fictitious and nominal independence. The financial circles concerned firmly believed—as did our political circles, who were more naïve than anything else—that it would be enough to give a few Congolese leaders titles of "Minister" or "Deputy," with decorations, luxury motorcars, big salaries, and splendid houses in the European quarter, in order to put a definite stop to the emancipation movement which threatened the financial interests.

Nevertheless, independence arrived with a flourish on June 30, 1960 when a ceremony was held in Léopoldville. The putative leaders of the new state mingled with the King of Belgium and the leaders of the major powers who had economic and political interests in the region.

The new Congolese head of state, President Joseph Kasavubu, exchanged diplomatic pleasantries with King Baudouin of Belgium. Wearing their best rose-tinted spectacles, both men spoke glowingly in their respective speeches of the relationship that existed between their two countries.

Caught in the joyous optimism of the moment and basking in the world's attention, President Kasavubu expressed the belief that this relationship would continue to grow.

Indeed, to usher in gently this era of respectful mutual cooperation between Léopoldville and the new Congo, a Treaty of Friendship had been signed by both states the previous day.

But before the Belgian administrators could gently pat themselves on the back for a job well done and go back to squeezing the Congo like a lemon, a discordant note was sounded.

The new Prime Minister, Patrice Lumumba, the former postman, was feeling heady in his new suit. He'd been a long time waiting, as had the other members of Congo's independence movement, the MNC, as they shuffled in the crowd that day.

When it came to Lumumba's turn to speak, he lashed the colonial administration as being a catalog of "atrocious sufferings, humiliating bondage, and filled with ironies, insults, [and] blows which we had to endure morning, noon, and night because we were Negroes."

Lumumba's words keenly articulate the gulf of understanding that was opening between the new native rulers and the ancient colonial regime.

One side believed the occasion was a little like letting the children have the run of the house, but putting padding on the sharp objects so no one got hurt. The adults would always be in attendance if things got out of hand.

The other side felt similar to the adolescent who longs for the opportunity to call his own shots and finally escapes out from under parental control.

As Capt. Dave Dignam wrote in a Command and Staff study carried out at the Irish Defence Force Military College, "The inauspicious birth of the Republic of the Congo was a prologue to disaster."

For those who had slept through Lumumba's speech, the wake-up call came only three days after the declaration of independence. Tribal strife exploded onto the streets of Léopoldville and in Luluabourg in the neighboring province of Kasaï.

Naturally, the Force Publique were deployed to restore order. Now renamed the Armée Nationale Congolaise (ANC), it failed to stop the violence.

The trouble that had broken out was due to tribal jockeying for position in the new order. While the white officers of the new ANC still gave orders, the landscape was not as clear under a native government.

Perhaps it was a fatal hesitation—a case of not wanting to be seen to do to your own what had previously been done by the colonizers. Perhaps it wasn't the new government's fault at all. Maybe the white officers, sensitive to the new political reality, were hesitant in their leadership.

Whatever was the cause, less than three days after independence, the rank and file of the ANC had become emboldened to such an extent that they rose against their European officers.

In the ensuing chaos, some fifty people were killed and three hundred injured. There was widespread damage and destruction to property, and most of the ten thousand Belgians living in the Congo were thrown into a state of mortal terror.

Naturally, there were appeals to the mother country to save them from being slaughtered in what was now a state filled with anarchy. Brussels responded by requesting the Congolese government to allow them to deploy Belgian troops stationed in the Congo to restore order. There were a large number of Belgian troops still in the Congo, particularly at Kamina Air Base in Katanga. The base was considered essential if required for NATO operations in Africa, and was also sited so the city could be used as an alternative Belgian capital in the event of a nuclear war in Europe.

Lumumba, rightly realizing that this was a real test of nationhood, refused to allow Belgian troops to roll out of their barracks to deal with the mutinous ANC. Unfortunately, this would probably have been the most effective expedient in restoring order, as the ANC could not be relied on in any significant numbers at this point.

Brussels tried for five days to get Lumumba to agree to their troops deploying, but to no avail. The ex-postman wasn't going back under the thumb, even if the house was coming down around his ears.

So Brussels did what any colonial power did in such circumstances. They sent in the troops anyway. A battalion of Belgian paratroopers was airlifted in to reinforce the troops already there.

The Belgian troops at Kamina, retained as part of a preindependence deal with the Congolese government, had already acted in concert with Katangan leaders and disarmed the local ANC forces.

But only in Katanga was an attempt made to recreate another indigenous security force to restore order.

What was to become known as the Katangan gendarmerie was established and ostensibly put under the command of an illiterate native ex-Force Publique sergeant major called Norbert Muké. However, the force was really controlled by Belgian officers.

The Belgian military deployment was regarded by the Congolese government as a violation of the much vaunted Treaty of Friendship. However, the damage had been done by the five-day lapse and, by the time the Belgians had left their bases, the mutinous ANC had consolidated their rampage.

The mayhem had now spread across the southern band of the country, taking in the provinces of Léopoldville and Kasaï. Then, more worryingly to the international forces of commerce, it spread to the mineral-rich Katanga.

Had the Belgians seized the initiative and restored order in the first days or, better still, created a native officer corps in the Force Publique before independence, the outbreak of violence may have been contained.

But now Brussels could do no more than throw more troops into the boiling pot. By July 19, only a few weeks after the filial declarations of Independence Day, the Belgians had committed ten thousand troops to the Congo.

For the Congolese government, it was difficult to see how things could have been worse. The country was in a worse uproar than it had ever been under the Belgians. Lumumba had totally lost control of his security forces.

Just when it seemed that the situation couldn't have gotten any worse for the fledgling State, it did.

Katanga, on which so many hopes were pinned, announced that they were pulling out of the deal. The Katangan position was articulated by their newly appointed leader, President Moise Tshombe. He stated that Lumumba was behaving like a Communist, and that in order to protect Katangan economic interests from the reigning Congo chaos, they were seceding.

Tshombe's supporters, it is interesting to note, were predominantly the white Belgians who had settled in Katanga and had extensive commercial interests there. He was also a favorite of the all-encroaching Union Minière.

This was a blow to the solar plexus of the Congo. While Katanga made up 10 percent of the Congolese population, it created a staggering 50 percent of the nation's revenue.

This declaration of independence forced Lumumba to turn to

the last hope he had of preserving any vestige of the Congo—the United Nations. He appealed for their help in imposing control over the virtually officerless ANC. Despite initially not wanting outside help, Lumumba was advised to take this course of action by the US Ambassador to the Congo, Clare H. Timberlake. Lumumba's hesitations about wanting foreign help were rapidly to dissolve after a number of other incidents.

In his study "Violence in the Congo; A Perspective of United Nations Peacekeeping," Major David R. Bloomer USMC declared that on July 11,

> three unrelated incidents touched off a new and more severe wave of violence. The first incident occurred in the port city of Matadi which was shelled by a Belgian warship. The shelling caused considerable damage and some loss of life. Meanwhile, Belgian paratroops quietly reinforced Belgian positions throughout the Congo. The Congolese army radio network carried exaggerated, hysterical versions of the paratroops' action. These broadcasts precipitated increased attacks on Europeans. On the same day, Tshombe made his move and declared Katanga to be a free and independent state.

This appeal to the UN by Lumumba had been made orally to Dr. Ralph Bunche, the UN representative in the Congo, and focused very much on the restoration of order. This was followed by another, more formal appeal in writing to the UN. Accompanying this were veiled threats to appeal to China if no help was forthcoming.

The appeal in writing to the UN Secretary-General, Dag Hammarskjöld, was much broader and more grandiose in its interpretation of events than Lumumba's earlier verbal appeal. It stated that the "external aggression and colonial machinations of Belgium [were a] threat to international peace and a violation of the recently signed Brussels–Léopoldville Treaty of Friendship."

The UN was then presented with a strife-ridden country, where the problems were being blamed on one hand on an uncontrollable paramilitary force, and on the other on interference by a European UN member state.

If this wasn't complicating things enough, Prime Minister Lumumba decided to internationalize the problem even further. Before a reply had been received from the UN, Lumumba and Kasavubu sent a telegram to the Soviet leader, Nikita Khrushchev. It read, "The Congo is occupied by Belgian troops and the lives of the Republic's president and prime minister are in danger."

Khruschev replied that the Soviets would render "any assistance that might be necessary for the victory of Congo's just cause." This was to have further consequences for both Lumumba and the Congo.

At this time, however, the UN Security Council—which, it should be noted, was working at unprecedented speed—passed a resolution authorizing military assistance for the Congo.

This became Security Council Resolution S/4387, adopted on July 14, 1960. It stated, "Considering the request for military assistance addressed to the Secretary-General by the President and the Prime Minister of the Congo, [the UN] calls upon the government of Belgium to withdraw their troops from the territory of the Republic of the Congo."

The Resolution also authorized the Secretary-General "to take the necessary steps, in consultation with the Government of the Republic of the Congo, to provide the Government with such military assistance as may be necessary until, through the effects of the Congolese Government with the technical assistance of the United Nations, the national security forces may be able, in the opinion of the Government, to meet fully their tasks."

The undertaking was titled Opération des Nations Unies au Congo, or United Nations Operation in the Congo. It became known as ONUC.

From the start the operation was fraught with organizational difficulties. Dag Hammarskjöld, the UN Secretary-General, believed UN Peacekeeping Operations needed to integrate the military, political, and economic forces at their disposal to reach their objective.

While essentially a good idea, this was initially to cause untold problems in the Congo regarding the command and deployment of UN troops.

At first a civilian UN appointee was chosen to head the entire UN operation, both civil and military. Then the arrival of British officer, Major Gen. H. T. Alexander, on secondment to command the Ghanaian UN battalion, ruffled UN feathers back in New York. Gen. Alexander, in the absence of any force commander, declared himself to be the temporary military commander.

UN Headquarters in New York responded by appointing Dr. Ralph Bunche, already in-country, to assume control of all UN forces. The first UN troops were to arrive in the Congo within forty-eight hours of Resolution S/4387 being passed, but the leadership was so confused that they soon found themselves being deployed willy-nilly throughout the country, without even the communications equipment to stay in touch.

In addition, most of the troops were briefed and equipped for what they perceived to be a police action, but which would rapidly degenerate into a miniwar to force Katanga back into the Congo.

It was into this maelstrom that Irish troops were about to march.

3

SEND IN THE IRISH

For where there are Irish there's bound to be fighting,
And when there's no fighting, it's Ireland no more!
—Rudyard Kipling,
"The Irish Guards"

Considering the timidity some Irish people now exhibit concerning involvement in Peace Support Operations, it seems that our confidence in them largely depends on who's running the show.

Recent debate about our involvement in the unmandated Battle Groups gave vent for those who choose hand-wringing, accompanied, of course, by moral angst, as their preferred form of daily aerobic exercise.

When one considers that the basic idea of the Battle Group is to give the UN a mechanism by which they can stabilize a situation with a well-trained interoperable force (that is, one capable of operating in an integrated fashion with another nation), it seems like good sense. But think about the Battle Group concept in the light of the lessons learned from earlier deployments like that of the Congo, and it seems imperative.

Although UN troops were swiftly to arrive in the Congo, landing there only two days after the resolution, they were by no means a cohesive force. In fact, the basic foundation for a military force in the field was nonexistent.

A position paper on the Congo UN operation from Waterloo University in Ontario, Canada, points out some of the special rules that were to curtail UN troops on operations:

In the next few weeks the Secretary-General developed his ground rules for the Congo operation ...

1. The Force was to be under the "exclusive command" of the Secretary-General, responsible only to the Security Council. It could not take orders from the host government and it "must be separate and distinct from activities of any national authorities."

2. The UN must not become a party to internal conflicts. UN troops could not be used to "enforce any specific political situation."

3. The Force must have freedom of movement throughout the Congo.

4. UN troops could use force only in self-defense and should not exercise "any initiative in the use of armed force."

5. The composition of the Force must be decided by the Secretary-General, although the views of the host country should be considered.

6. National units in the UN Force should take orders only from the UN and not from their governments.

Any force to have a measure of success needs clear mission objectives. It needs a defined structure of what in military terms is referred to as C3—or Command, Control, and Communications.

The troops who arrived in the Congo were lightly armed. They were equipped and briefed for what can best be described as a police-type action—that is, restoration of law and order, and dealing with recalcitrant members of the mutinous ANC.

By July 15, more than 1,200 troops were on the ground, and within a month the total had soared to 14,000 men from twenty-four member states. In terms of numbers and the scope of the mission, a task of unprecedented magnitude was under way. But whether or not the United Nations could control such a force was as yet undetermined.

However, the root of the original difficulties of July and August 1960 lay in the erratic personality of Patrice Lumumba. There seemed little doubt at the time that Lumumba was under the influence of certain Communist advisors. Even Hammarskjöld believed this.

Certainly, the Prime Minister showed little interest in cooperating with the UN in its efforts to restore order from the chaos of the Congo. The first real difficulty arose over the problem of the secessionist province of Katanga.

There, President Moise Tshombe, with the assistance of Belgian officers and civilian advisors, had established an oasis of relative tranquility. Tshombe persistently refused to admit UN troops, and Lumumba demanded that the UN Forces expel the Belgians from Katanga and compel Tshombe to end his secession. Hammarskjöld could not do this, however, without violating all his ground rules for ONUC.

The result was that the Secretary-General personally led the first ONUC contingent into Katanga. But this action, while demonstrating the UN's right to freedom of movement, did nothing to resolve the political impasse.

The ONUC force was certainly a polyglot one, comprising members hailing from Argentina, Austria, Brazil, Burma, Canada, Ceylon, Denmark, Ethiopia, Ghana, Guinea, India, Indonesia, Iran, Ireland, Italy, Liberia, Malaya, Federation of Mali, Morocco, Netherlands, Nigeria, Norway, Pakistan, Philippines, Sierra Leone, Sudan, Sweden, Tunisia, United Arab Republic, and Yugoslavia.

Cultural, linguistic, and economic factors were also to be major issues in trying to lead and administer such a force efficiently.

Added to the complexity of the tasks ahead was the attitude of the host country whom the UN were supposed to be assisting. Documents compiled by Canadian staff officers of the time show that

> while the Congo government invited the UN to come in their country to establish law and order and restore the economic life, the Prime Minister and at least some of his colleagues are antagonistic to white troops in particular and to the UN forces generally.

> It is becoming more obvious with each passing day that a police state is in the making and the pressure of the UN is a deterrent to the process.

Ireland had already seconded troops to the UN by 1960, but this was in the low-profile capacity of unarmed observers to truce supervision missions in the Middle East.

So, when the request arrived from UN Headquarters in New York to supply a full infantry battalion, military planners at Defence Force Headquarters (DFHQ) knew it would be a watershed in Irish military history.

To appreciate fully the magnitude of what was being asked of the Irish Army, one must understand the state of the Irish military in the late 1950s.

In the words of Lieutenant Noel Carey, then a young, enthusiastic platoon commander, the Army

> was run down, lacked financing and direction, and its mission was not clearly defined. Duties consisted of ceremonial training and Aid to the Civil Power, as the IRA border campaign was beginning at the time.
>
> I spent a three-month period on the border and at least there we were carrying out essential duties, setting up roadblocks and patrols with the gardaí. The work was interesting and demanding.
>
> Once back in barracks however, the tedium was worse than ever. Sport was very important to me and was a help in keeping me motivated, as I was involved in soccer, rugby, basketball, GAA, and athletics. However, there was a distinct lack of adventure in the army at this time.

His words sum up the reality for many Irish soldiers of that period. For some, the army was simply a staging post, a chance to earn and save money before they headed off to pastures greener in the US or Australia. For others it was simply a straightforward way to keep a roof over their heads and feed their families.

At any rate, a glorious career it was not.

At this point there would have been very few Irish soldiers that would have seen active service. A small number of senior officers who still served had seen some action in the War of Independence and later the Civil War.

However, tactics and maneuver of troops had changed substantially since then. While there were a number, particularly among the NCO corps, who had seen action serving with the British forces in

World War II, the truth was that in military terms, the Irish Army was a virgin.

Neville, one of the senior NCOs that served with A Company, remembered well the number of ex-British Army men that were serving in the Irish Army when he enlisted in the 1930s:

> At that time lots of the NCO corps were Irishmen who had served in World War I, lots of them had been in regiments like the Irish Guards and some had been in the corps units. They were all very experienced soldiers.

> I remember one who was an ex-Royal Artillery man. He was an instructor in the Curragh Camp. They really were terrific instructors and great soldiers. I often remember being on courses where they would start reminiscing about incidents during the War of Independence or the Rising.

> One fellow recalled carrying James Connolly out of the GPO, but we were never sure which side he'd been on. So many of them had fought during World War I and then came home to join the IRA, and some had ended up fighting against the rebels at the GPO before they were shipped off to France. But they all seemed to get on with each other in the Irish Army.

In 1960 the Army only numbered in the region of seven thousand troops. This was a minuscule number with which to provide even the basic requirements for a peacetime army in a democratic society.

The end of World War II had seen a massive downsizing of the Army, as most who had enlisted had done so only for the duration of the war, or "Emergency" as it was known in Ireland. They were known as E men.

The seven-thousand-strong Army was scattered all over the country in a series of depleted and half-formed units. The Army was in a state of terminal stagnation, and combating the IRA border campaign, as evidenced from Noel Carey's recollection, was the only duty it was fulfilling.

Coupled with the stagnation and lack of battle experience was the scarce finances for realistic training. At a time when armies around the world were gradually being prepared for counter-insurgency operations or full-blown conventional operations in Europe, Irish troops' basic training was heavy on square bashing, marksmanship, and the obligatory spit and polish.

Equipment was World War II vintage at best, and in many cases still World War I. Looking at the uniform and equipment of Irish troops in 1960 it would be easy to mistake them for British Tommies going to the front in 1914.

Indeed, it wasn't just the uniform that was reminiscent of the old British Army. The way of life and discipline was too. Former Sgt. Walter Hegarty, DSM, recalls enlisting in the 1950s when the Defence Act had just been implemented:

When I look back I realize how tough it was, but then I was delighted when I joined up. I had left a job as a part-time postal worker to get a job with a regular income, uniform, food, and lodgings provided.

I had been ill in my late teens, but I was now fit and up for anything. Even though the uniform was not terribly glamorous, we used to take every opportunity to spruce it up when we went into town.

At the time there were many auld sweats in Galway Barracks who told me I was joining at an easy time. Before the Defence

Act came in you could be charged with a thing called Mute of Malice or Dumb Insolence. It basically meant an NCO or officer could have you charged because you were being maliciously silent when asked a question ... even if it was one you just didn't know the answer to.

It was just a way [of] instilling fear and discipline into us. The Army was a rigid system and you got used to that fact early on, or got out.

The army that Carey, Neville, and Hegarty were existing in was doing its best to attend to its duties and keep itself in a state to carry out whatever missions were assigned it. But it was a struggle to remain enthusiastic. When volunteers were looked for to fill a battalion to go to Africa, there was no shortage of them.

From privates to colonels, everyone thought the Congo mission a heaven-sent opportunity. As is always the case with professional soldiers, the chance to go on active service was a great lure. For the general staff at DFHQ, the planning focused on sending a reinforced company of 250 men when the first tentative request came for troops.

When the request for a battalion comprising around 700 men came, the general staff, rather than shy away, readily agreed, knowing this was the much needed shot in the arm the Army needed.

They also felt sure now that the mandarins in the Department of Finance would send some much-needed budgetary assistance the Army's way.

The UN request was agreed to on July 15, 1960, and twelve days later, Col. Murt Buckley led the men of the 32nd Battalion out to Baldonnel Aerodrome for their transport to the Congo.

And what about the hoped-for money from the Department of Finance? Well, even if troops are conditioned to move hastily on short notice, this is not the case with the civil service—particularly a civil service coming out of the moribund 1950s.

So it came to pass that the first Irish soldiers to embark on overseas active service in Africa did so in bullswool uniforms and hob-nailed boots with bolt-action rifles. Veterans recall the bemusement of the American airmen who landed at Baldonnel to fly them to Africa.

"We got some looks, all right," recalls John Gorman.

The United States Air Force (USAF) crew, having arrived in state-of-the-art Globemaster transport aircraft, must have thought they had stepped back in time as they looked at the Irish troops file aboard.

President Éamon De Valera was there, along with the Army Chief of Staff, to see the troops off. So it was for the 32nd Battalion, and so it would be for five more Irish battalions that would see action in Africa.

Some of the Irish veterans recall, bizarrely, being mistaken for Koreans when they came off the plane, such was the confusion of the Americans at their attire and equipment.

While the 32nd Battalion were en route to the Congo, a further request came from the UN for more Irish troops. Within three weeks of the 32nd Battalion's departure, the seven-hundred-strong 33rd Battalion was flying out.

The number of Irish troops serving on an overseas mission to Africa now totaled just under 1,500, including all ranks and attachments. At a later stage, the entire ONUC force, numbering 20,000 men at its peak, was to be commanded by an Irish officer, Lt. Gen. Sean McKeown.

But at this time, Major Gen. Carl von Horn, a Swedish officer, had taken the reins of leadership following the initial confusion about who was to be the senior ONUC military officer.

The problem for von Horn was that he had to operate in a situation where the ONUC military leadership was being hamstrung by the UN civilian leadership who made operational decisions they were ill equipped to make.

ONUC comprised both a military (von Horn) and civil

wing. The heads of both operations were subordinate to a Special Representative (Dr. Ralph Bunche) who in turn reported the UN Secretary-General (Hammarskjöld).

This created major tensions for von Horn. Upon arrival at Léopoldville, he was to find the military side of the mission in total chaos.

ONUC and its military staff planners seemed completely incapable of filling the vacuum created by the quick departure of the Belgian government and there was intense need for an international force to restore order.

In a subsequent book on his peacekeeping experiences, *Soldiering for Peace,* von Horn emphasizes how difficult his mission was made, particularly by the poor facilities and poor communications.

Even his transfer from the United Nations Truce Supervision Organisation (UNTSO) in the Middle East had difficulties, in that the aircraft flying him to Africa broke down. He finally arrived on July 18.

Von Horn objected to certain decisions of the UN political leadership, which he felt were degrading his force's ability to conduct military operations. So strongly did the Swede feel about this that he threatened to resign on three separate occasions in the month following his arrival to the Congo. The first occasion was after UN Secretary-General Hammarskjöld turned down a request for a larger force to implement the UN resolution S/4387. The second crisis erupted when von Horn discovered that all of his communications were being filtered through a civilian sieve before reaching their destination at UN Headquarters in New York. But the straw that nearly broke the camel's back, and consequently was to cause morale and operational problems for the ONUC troops on the ground, was the decision to return arms previously seized from errant ANC units in UN raids.

Added to these complications was the increasingly erratic and hostile attitude of the Congolese government to the ONUC forces. A state of martial law was declared by August, with demands that all

UN personnel, civil and military, must carry ID and produce it on request to the Congolese authorities.

This and other awkward and demeaning regulations can be interpreted as the flailing of an immature state trying to assert its authority on a situation that had increasingly spiraled out of its control. However, it certainly impeded the conduct of ONUC operations to restore order and stability throughout the Congo.

Canadian staff officers at the ONUC Headquarters in reports home stated that ONUC was "primarily a civilian organization with a military component." The reports continue:

Starting with a handful of UN officials under Dr. Bunche and a small group of officers, mostly Canadian, borrowed from UNEF [United Nations Emergency Force] and UNTSO, this organization has mushroomed into a tremendous and awesome establishment, lacking cohesion, know-how, and any real practical authority. For weeks, civilians, officers, and other ranks have been pouring in from all over the world; people who have little in common and who are tied by strings which prevent or restrict their use. This rapid expansion of HQ ONUC, seemingly without any plan, has resulted in most of the effort being directed at their own administration to the detriment of the eighteen thousand troops spread over a territory as large as the whole of Ontario but without its means of communications. This situation, together with an almost total lack of telephonic communication between offices and an impossible accommodation set up has caused intolerable delay, confusion, and frustration right from the start, and the end is not yet in sight.

Not surprisingly, by late 1960, von Horn was in ill health and had withdrawn more and more from the operational decision-making arena. His senior staff officers were despairing of focused leadership. By December of that year, von Horn had returned to UNTSO and a new force commander was appointed.

In January 1961, Lt. Gen. Sean McKeown was appointed Force Commander to ONUC. Formerly Chief of Staff to the Irish Defence Forces, McKeown was a seen as a popular choice by all the nations serving in ONUC.

The smaller states were happy to see an officer from a state with a noncolonial background in the position, and the larger western states were happy to serve under an officer of a similar cultural background who could speak their language, both literally and operationally.

The net result was a huge boost for Irish Army morale, which only increased applications from Irish servicemen to be part of the Congo operation.

The Irish battalions that arrived in the Congo were to take up their duties at Elisabethville, the capital of the breakaway province of Katanga.

Katanga at this stage was somewhat more stable than the rest of the Congo. Moise Tshombe, the newly proclaimed president, had the benefit of the mercenary-led gendarmerie to keep order and defend against a rampaging ANC.

While this initially meant a comparatively straightforward transition for the Irish battalions to African service, it was this same gendarmerie that was to lead to many Irish headaches and heartaches in days to come.

A Company was not to arrive in-country until April 1961, by which time a number of incidents involving Irish troops had taken place.

The most infamous, and the one which had the greatest effect on the perception of the Irish public, was Niemba, which happened on November 8, 1960.

Niemba was an isolated trading post on the river Lukuga in Katanga. It was typical of UN operations at the time in that it was of no real tactical importance.

Nine Irish soldiers, including the platoon commander, Lt. Kevin Gleeson, were slaughtered south of Niemba by marauding Baluba tribesmen. This action was to have a number of effects on how the general public viewed the unfolding events in the Congo.

While the Baluba attack on Gleeson's platoon was undoubtedly unprovoked and ferocious, the Baluba generally were on the receiving end of aggression.

A primitive tribal people, they had been regularly terrorized and abused by the mercenary-led forces in Katanga. Many Baluba tribespeople had gone to Elisabethville, where ironically, they were to be protected by Irish and other UN forces.

It is likely that the attack at Niemba was a knee-jerk reaction by a primitive people who had already been terrorized by forces led by whites. Both the Katangans and the Balubas were constantly blaming the UN for siding with one or the other faction.

The attack happened after Irish troops were instructed to go out and remove roadblocks that had been set up by the Balubas. It was while doing this they were set upon. Studies and reports since then acknowledge that had there been greater intelligence resources available to the ONUC, it would have been clear an attack was imminent.

If proof were needed of ONUC's lack of operational knowledge of where they were deploying troops, Niemba proved it. After the massacre the UN withdrew from the area.

In any event, the plethora of newspaper stories about the arrow-pierced bodies of the troops recovered after the Niemba massacre fed into the mindsets of the general public. As far as the Irish public was concerned, their troops were fighting a savage but ignorant force armed with stone-age weapons.

The general feeling was that the Irish soldiers had died because they did not want to intimidate or take aggressive action. Surely this would never happen again. They wouldn't be caught out in such a manner.

However, it was the well-armed, mercenary-led Katangan forces who would be the main enemy Irish troops were to face during their time in the Congo, and the reluctance to make the first move would prove a crucial problem.

There was no question that the Katangan forces were the military equal of any European force ranged against them and, in the initial stages of the Katangan secession, were much better equipped than the Irish.

The Katangan gendarmerie, despite its name, was really a military and not a police force. Following the secession of Katanga and their successes in disarming the threat of the ANC rabble, it was the Baluba tribes dominating North Katanga that presented the most significant threat to Katangan stability.

Bands of Baluba youths had formed into loose gangs called La Jeunesse. This title was eventually to inspire terror in both white and black alike.

As uneducated youths disaffected by the Katangan regime, La Jeunesse had no real political outlook, and were just taking advantage of the anarchy that reigned since independence.

They weren't particularly well armed by military standards, but roaming the countryside with their sharpened bicycle chains and panga knives, they made the white settlers uneasy.

President Tshombe would come to rely heavily on seconded Belgian officers such as Col. Crèvecoeur to command and train his gendarmerie and turn it into a bulwark against the civil disorder threatening his breakaway state.

A Belgian para brigade arrived in Katanga to assist in restoring order in July after independence was declared. But in accordance with the UN resolution, the Belgians recalled their troops soon afterwards.

However, a number of Belgian officers and NCOs stayed on with the gendarmerie. This was to be the start of the mercenary influx into Katanga that was to cause the UN such headaches.

Col. Guy Weber, formerly of the Belgian paras, became President Tshombe's military adviser and became active organizing other Belgian settlers and former officers in the new Katangan military.

Another Belgian, Col. Carlos Huyghe, is reputed to be the first one to suggest to President Tshombe that he actively start hiring white mercenaries from wherever possible.

By the end of 1960, the war between the gendarmerie and the Balubas in North Katanga had become nasty and was getting out of control. In addition, havoc was being created by ANC deserters who were spilling into North Katanga and bringing whatever weapons and military ordinances they could with them. ONUC forces were still settling in and were too isolated in small pockets with imperfect communications to try and bring any real stability to the situation on the ground.

President Tshombe was now open to any suggestions that would enable him to keep his state intact. At this point he was under a certain amount of pressure from foreign commercial interests to stabilize the situation in mineral-rich Katanga and preserve its status.

However, it was the beefing up of his gendarmerie that was to bring him into direct conflict with the UN and with the Irish troops who were stuck in the heart of Katanga. At first, the UN ignored the arrival of mercenary forces, and an uneasy truce existed between the UN and Katangan forces. President Tshombe had threatened to use force when Swedish UN troops entered Katanga on August 12, 1960, but the threat never turned into reality.

It would be fair to say that at this stage, the UN, in particular Secretary-General Hammarskjöld, had his hands full in dealing with the Congolese government and trying to restrain Prime Minister

Lumumba from taking military action against Katanga.

The Congolese Prime Minister was getting increasingly erratic at this stage and had come into conflict with President Kasavubu, who tried to sack his wayward Prime Minister. Lumumba replied by sacking President Kasavubu.

This chaotic state of affairs was to be added to by the Chief of Staff of the ANC, Gen. Joseph Mobutu, who would later lead the Congo and bleed it dry until he died of cancer while living in luxury in Europe. He dissolved the Government and took power, then he appointed a team of commissioners who, under his direction, would run the country. Of course, the UN refused to recognize this state of affairs. Against this surreal backdrop, the UN troops still had to try and operate on the ground.

Lumumba's erratic behavior and the arrival of mercenaries were to precipitate a number of events. By 1961, he had denounced the Belgians, the Katangans and the UN for being one-sided, and he had commenced calling on the Soviets and Czechs for military aid. It was probably this that finally sealed his fate.

Following Mobutu's seizure of power, Lumumba, after being humiliated and beaten in public, was put on a plane to Katanga.

This apparently was done at Belgian insistence, as they knew Tshombe's regime would finally remove this troublesome anticolonial thorn from their side. According to a recent book by Belgian sociologist Ludo de Witte, *The Assassination of Lumumba*, Belgium's African Affairs Minister, Harold d'Aspremont Lynden, ordered that Lumumba be flown to Katanga.

At this time, many natives believed Belgian mercenaries were responsible for his death. After another severe beating on the plane, Lumumba was eventually to die by a firing squad on January 17, 1961, under the orders of the native-led Katagan government. The irony was that, although the firing squad was commanded by a Belgian officer, it was native Africans who ordered his death.

According to those in Elisabethville at the time, it was Godefroid Munongo, one of Tshombe's ministers, who took a soldier's bayonet and drove it into Lumumba's chest while the two exchanged taunts.

Conor Cruise O'Brien, who in June of that year was to take over the ONUC operation in Katanga as the Special Representative of the UN Secretary-General, later wrote of Munongo: "I should not like to encounter very often in dreams...Godfroid [sic] Munongo's dark spectacles...it is generally believed in Elisabethville that he killed Lumumba with his own hands."

A Belgian mercenary named Ruys is reputed to have administered a coup de grace to Lumumba as he lay dying.

However, this grisly episode was not yet finished for the Belgian colonialists. They now had to destroy the evidence. Four days later, Gerard Soete, the Belgian Commissioner of the Katangan Police, along with his brother, cut up the hapless body of Lumumba with a hacksaw and dissolved it in sulphuric acid.

In an interview on Belgian television last year, Soete displayed a bullet and two teeth he claimed to have saved from Lumumba's body. Soete and his brother also had to burn some of the remains that the acid didn't destroy. The two men carried out their duty while steaming drunk on whiskey, such was the horror of the task.

In February 1961, the UN proclaimed another resolution. This one allowed the UN to use force to restore order and take whatever steps were necessary to prevent civil war erupting in the Congo. The resolution also demanded the immediate evacuation of all mercenaries and other foreign military and political advisers.

It was this resolution that led to the first of the significant UN operations involving Irish troops. The road was cleared to Operation Rumpunch, and with it A Company's steps into UN history.

4

THE MERCENARY EQUATION

Cry, "Havoc," and let slip the dogs of war.

—William Shakespeare,

Julius Caesar

The 35th Battalion, of which A Company was part, was not to arrive in the Congo until June 1961, nearly a year after UN troops were first committed. But during A Company's six-month tour of duty in the Congo, two of the pivotal operations that defined the nature and direction of ONUC's strategy took place.

In order to understand how the Congo became a major news event and a defining chapter in UN peacekeeping history, one must understand the conditions that led to Operation Rumpunch and its progeny, Operation Morthor. For it was these operations that led to what became known as the second battle of Katanga, and the siege at Jadotville. It also requires an understanding of the precursor actions for both operations which led to a descent into outright war rather than the "police actions" originally envisaged for the ONUC force when it was deployed to the Congo.

One of the single most distinguishing features that led to Katangan and UN forces coming into conflict was the addition of mercenary officers to the Katangan forces, for the on-the-ground tactics and military strategy of the Katangan secession were generally conceived and executed by these largely Belgian and French officers.

The period following Lumumba's death, between January and June of 1961, had seen a continuing deterioration of order throughout the Congo.

On August 2, Mr. Cyrille Adoula was elected to replace the murdered Lumumba as Prime Minister of the Congo. Within twenty-four hours he announced his intention to end the Katangan secession.

Special legislation was enacted to allow the Congolese government to expel foreign officers and mercenaries. This move was to have massive ramifications for the Congo and the UN, for in moving against the foreign officers and mercenaries, Adoula called on the UN's assistance.

The UN now had a mandate that allowed for force to be used in the pursuit of such an objective. Thus their assistance was granted, and the UN was pulled into the internal factional fighting of the Congo— something neither it nor its participating members such as Ireland had ever intended.

At this point, the secession of Katanga was being seen as the single biggest obstacle to restoring order to the Congo. And within Katanga, it was the development of the gendarmerie that was proving the single biggest force in propelling the Congo towards civil war.

As already mentioned, the Katangan gendarmerie's robust response to the Baluba and other elements such as the ANC deserters had created more problems than it solved.

In the early stages of 1961, Hammarskjöld and the UN labored to reconcile Tshombe's Katanga and the Congolese government, but to no avail. Chief amongst the reasons for the lack of entente was the sheer growth of the Katangan forces.

This growth was achieved largely through the recruitment of mercenary troops of all ranks. Initially the officers had been Belgians on secondment. But following the second UN resolution, these officers and career NCOs returned to their duties in Europe.

When the recruitment of mercenaries was first accepted by Tshombe, centers for their induction were opened in Southern Rhodesia at Bulawayo and Salisbury. Tentatively at first, advertisements started to appear in the local press offering well-paid openings for "police officers" in the Katangan gendarmerie.

Word rapidly spread throughout the Federation of Rhodesia that Katanga was recruiting. It was also accepted that the Federation's then leader, Sir Roy Welensky, tacitly supported this. Indeed, Welensky was to become a friend and supporter of Tshombe, believing Katanga's survival necessary for the continued stability being enjoyed in the Federation.

While this led to a steady trickle of white Rhodesians with military experience across the border into the Katangan ranks, it was not nearly enough to plug the gap left by the Belgians.

Tshombe realized this. He decided to keep with Francophone tradition and expand his recruiting base to include French officers and NCOs. Rather than simply send emissaries to trawl the bars in Marseilles for former Foreign Legionnaires now kicked out of Algeria, Tshombe made a secret request to no less a personage than French premier, Gen. Charles de Gaulle.

France was not averse to extending its web of influence into a large French-speaking chunk of Africa. In fact, de Gaulle was to authorize Col. Roger Trinquier, an officer who had cut his command teeth leading a regiment of colonial paras in Algeria, covertly to organize French assistance to Katanga.

However, Trinquier was more than just an able officer with

special warfare knowledge. He was widely regarded by professional military officers as an expert in matters of insurgency from his service as a behind-the-lines operator in Vietnam.

However, it was during his Algerian service that he became infamous in international military circles for pioneering torture in counter-insurgency operations. His involvement showed how seriously the French were viewing their assistance, albeit covert, to Katanga.

On January 25, 1961, Col. Trinquier arrived and assumed total command of the Katangan gendarmerie. Accompanying the Colonel when he strode into Elisabethville airport were a number of other French officers, including Comdt. Robert Falques. To get a measure of the men now organizing and leading the Katangan forces, it should be realized that Falques was formerly an officer in the 1er Regiment Étranger de Parachutistes, or the 1st Foreign Legion Parachute Regiment.

This unit, after he had left, was to be disbanded in disgrace following its involvement in the attempted putsch against de Gaulle on account of his policy on Algeria. Most of its officers and senior NCOs ended up in prison as a result.

Falques had a reputation for being lucky and tough, not only because of his timely move from the Foreign Legion to Katanga, but also because he had survived the prison camps of the Viet Minh following France's disastrous adventure in Vietnam.

Col. Trinquier's first act as commanding officer of Tshombe's forces was to present him with a written analysis that the main threat to Katanga would be from revolutionary cells organized in the Katangan capital, Elisabethville. In fact, many other foreign influences, both state and commercial, were to be guilty of fearing the potency of these revolutionaries. They thus provided the support for Katanga to prosecute its war of secession.

But when one looks back at what eventually was to ring the

death knell for Katanga's brief chapter of statehood, you might be inclined to think that Trinquier was completely mad. Katanga would eventually be suppressed by the forces of ONUC fighting conventional infantry battles, and these "revolutionary cells" entirely failed to give any real trouble to the nascent state, if they weren't just a figment of Trinquier's battle-scarred imagination.

There was method in his madness when he presented this apparently spurious report. He assured an already jittery Tshombe that to combat the "revolutionary cells" he would need to up to twenty more French officers experienced in counter-insurgency warfare. The autocratic Trinquier also insisted on being given complete command for up to five years of the gendarmerie, all Belgian officers still in the gendarmerie, the Ministry of Information, and the Ministry of the Interior.

While he was on a roll, the charismatic colonel also demanded the full and unbridled support of President Tshombe. He then told Tshombe, "Alone in fact, I will be no use to you. It is necessary then, on this point at least, that I should obtain the aid and support of the French government."

In effect, Trinquier was demanding a complete French takeover of Katanga. Tshombe wished the Colonel "Godspeed" on his recruiting trip back to France and promised his enthusiastic support.

However, the previously mentioned Belgian Col. Weber, who had elected to stay on after the other Belgian troops left, had also been promised support from an ever-enthusiastic Tshombe. The separatist president eventually dealt with this problem by refusing Trinquier and his plane-load of French mercenaries permission to land in Katanga. The plane was diverted to Northern Rhodesia where Trinquier would be entangled in negotiations with the Minister of the Interior, Godefroid Munongo.

However, Trinquier was to be luckier than Lumumba in his meeting with Munongo, suffering only dented pride as he received word that his services were no longer required.

The other French officers, though, elected to stay on in Katanga and Comdt. Falques became their leader. In fact, he got Trinquier's job, and became the military leader of Katanga and probably the main cause of Katanga's initial ability to fight off the ONUC forces.

Falques was the archetypal mercenary leader—tough and ruthless. He even sported a number of colorful scars from his Vietnam days. He was quietly admired by professional soldiers as a resourceful and charismatic leader. He was to find a number of able assistants in the mercenaries that arrived in Katanga. They ranged from extreme to extreme, in both physical appearance and background.

One of these was the indefatigable Bob Denard, a former NCO who had fought in the French Marines in Indochina. Denard was a tall, mustachioed man with a complicated past—which included a fourteen-month stretch in prison for his involvement in a plot to assassinate a French politician in 1954.

It was in the last battle for Katanga against UN forces that Denard was to gain a reputation as a mercenary leader.

One of the other leading mercenary leaders emerging couldn't have been more different. Jean "Black Jack" Schramme, scion of a wealthy Belgian family, had come to the Congo at eighteen to run the family's plantation near the capital of the Orientale province, Stanleyville.

Like many Belgian settlers, he had fled after the declaration of Congolese independence but returned in early 1961 to become a training officer with the Katangan gendarmerie. In the early struggle to secure recruits for the gendarmerie he raised a force of fifteen- to seventeen-year-olds from local tribes in North Katanga, which he commanded as the "Leopard Group." Now that Katanga was no longer a client state of France, she needed skilled fighting men to prevent the UN from forcing her back into the Congo. Again, France was to provide the nucleus of this force, albeit inadvertently.

The failed coup against de Gaulle in April 1961, led by elements of the Foreign Legion and colonial forces, made for a steady flow of battle-hardened ex-French colonial soldiers arriving in Katanga.

By this point, two distinct mercenary elements were forming in Katanga—a Francophone component consisting of Belgians and French, and an Anglophone one made up of disparate Rhodesian, South African, and British expat adventurers. Coincidentally, this also included a number of Irish.

While the Belgians and French distrusted each other and even fought amongst themselves, they would always band together when dealing with the Anglophones. The French-speakers certainly went on to earn the less savory reputation of the two groups. They became known by the natives as *les affreux*, which translates as "the terrors."

Both groups came together to form what was initially known as the Compagnie Internationale. This unit earned a reputation similar to that of the Black and Tan units that terrorized Ireland from 1920. It was such a force that was to come into battle with A Company at Jadotville some months later.

It wasn't long before the now mercenary-infused Katangan forces clashed with the UN. On April 7, 1961, at Manono in Northern Katanga, shooting broke out between several Anglophone mercenaries and troops from ONUC's Ethiopian contingent.

A number of the Ethiopians were killed in the engagement, and approximately thirty mercenaries, including their CO, an Englishman named Capt. Richard Browne, were captured.

The UN were now to take cognizance of the effect of the escalating influx of mercenaries, following a report by a UN official, Dr. Mekki Abbas. Dr. Abbas confirmed that

the non-Congolese military personnel formed the back-bone of the military operations in Katanga and were instrumental in carrying out the recent offensive of the Katangan forces.

In particular, the Compagnie Internationale commanded by Capt. Browne and composed of experienced and disciplined soldiers seemed to have supplied the elite necessary for this type of operation.

So while the Irish public still cultivated notions of their troops going out to fight savage but primitive tribesmen, the newly arrived troops of the 35th Battalion were facing into action with a well-led light infantry force.

Operation Rumpunch would be the beginning of the UN and Katanga coming into direct confrontation. Curiously enough, the UN thought the operation would have the opposite effect. Their operational conception was that Rumpunch would remove the individuals that were prolonging secession and bringing Katanga into open conflict with the UN. Previously, UN forces in the Congo had been constrained by the initial resolution, being limited only to defensive actions. However, when the resolution changed, it coincided with a number of other changes in senior personnel in ONUC.

By June 1961, there was a new head of UN operations in Katanga, Irish diplomat Conor Cruise O'Brien. O'Brien was faced with the seemingly impossible job of coordinating all UN activities— diplomatic, military, and development—throughout Katanga. He was described in *The New Mercenaries* by historian Anthony Mockler as "a belligerent Irishman of very decided political views," which paints O'Brien in stage-Irish mode, as the temperamental, stubborn Irishman, and is probably a little unfair.

A cursory glance at his own Congo story, *To Katanga and Back*, certainly demonstrates O'Brien to be a resolute character with no delusions regarding the immensity and complexity of the task that lay before him.

In addition to O'Brien taking the helm in Katanga, the military reins of the ONUC had passed onto Lt. Gen. Sean McKeown. Some, such as Mockler, seem to suggest that this was fortunate for O'Brien. In his own book, O'Brien accepts that this was the case and made settling in easier—not because McKeown was a fellow Irishman, but rather because he was a consummate professional soldier who was managing to knock some shape onto the amorphous and disparate ONUC contingents. O'Brien says:

> I had not known General McKeown very well before in Ireland, but I knew the high and steady reputation which he had in a country which is no great respecter of persons, especially of those who—like Generals—need, in the opinions of their countrymen, to be saved from the dread disease of a "swelled head."

> Certainly Sean McKeown has been entirely spared that affliction. He is the kind of soldier Tolstoy liked: modest, tough, and realistic.

O'Brien succinctly adds a caveat that his praise of McKeown should not be interpreted as Irish chauvinism on his part, pointing out Dr. Johnson's aphorism: "The Irish are a fair people—they never speak well of one another."

This, incidentally, was a truism later to be borne out in the aftermath of Jadotville. Whatever way one views it, one must admit that McKeown's reputation was well-deserved, when it is understood what an uphill struggle he had begun.

Unlike a general serving, say, the Allies in World War II, or even a NATO general in the Cold War, McKeown was trying to apply military solutions to rather vague and sometimes contradictory instructions from UN Headquarters in New York. As O'Brien puts it, "He had, for discharging the multifarious and ill-defined tasks laid down by the Security Council and Assembly, in a turbulent country over four times as large as France, a mixed force about one-third the size of the homogenous force with which the British Government had attempted, unsuccessfully, to 'maintain order' in the tiny island of Cyprus."

Added to the physical problems of stabilizing the Congo was the difficult and politically sensitive nature of McKeown's planning staff. Anyone with military service will understand that the officers a commanding general has to assist him are crucial in formulating strategy and seeing that it gets implemented by the forces in the field.

The staff officers are the ones who act as additional hands and eyes for the general. Usually a general will have built up his staff over a number of years. This will usually comprise bright up-and-coming officers who, in addition to being professionally competent, will be attuned to the personality and nuances of their boss. Such sensitivity under times of stress can make the difference between success and failure.

McKeown had to labor with a number of appointments that were made purely to satisfy the political demands of the UN. While there were some Canadian, a few Irish, and a number of well-regarded Indian officers, there were a number whose military education and poor English skills would have made for difficult communications.

There were also a number of officers who would have privately questioned McKeown's judgement, because of his lack of previous war service and their own professional jealousy. It was against this backdrop that the first significant operation of ONUC was being planned—Operation Rumpunch.

One of the first tenets of any military operation is the provision of good intelligence. Without it the commander cannot carry out what in military parlance is termed an Estimate of the Situation (Est. of Sit.) or an Appreciation of the Ground. And aside from purely military applications, it gives a commander an understanding of things such as enemy morale, local civilian morale, and therefore prospective cultural interpretation of certain military strategies.

Even more importantly, good intelligence acts as a force multiplier for any military operation in areas such as devising or countering propaganda or psychological operations. Intelligence used in such a fashion may often achieve objectives with a minimum blood-loss.

Intelligence must be examined from both a strategic and tactical point of view. Simply put, the information gathered will be used to make decisions by commanders such as McKeown to devise operations, and by commanders on the ground in implementation of these operations.

What was the UN's intelligence-gathering capability at this time? There was a small ONUC Military Information Branch organized to collate intelligence, but it was given very little resources and did not handle agents as such. However, perhaps Conor Cruise O'Brien can paint a more vivid picture of what in ONUC passed for an intelligence-gathering function.

Referring to Swedish Col. Jonas Waern and a report he delivered on the situation in Elisabethville prior to the execution of Operation Rumpunch, O'Brien recalls:

> He referred to several items of information as having been gleaned from "my spies." Now this touches on a sensitive point, where the United Nations operation in the Congo is concerned. Individual powers supporting the UN operation did maintain intelligence networks, but the UN itself did not. Hammarskjöld had referred to this once at a meeting of the Congo Advisory Committee...[He] admitted that it was a serious handicap and had justified the lack on the grounds that the UN must "have clean hands."

O'Brien rightly observes that trying to institute such a service would be fraught with difficulties. The problem of trying to observe the necessary tight security between so many different nations was augmented by the practical difficulties of different languages.

Further to this was the rather naïve and childish argument that intelligence gathering would leave the way open to "the sort of things intelligence services habitually do—lying, bribery, blackmail, theft, and so on."

Apparently the UN also agonized over the notion that such an intelligence service would be subject to "infiltration by agents of national services"—which, all-in-all, provides a stunning argument for not having a UN force committed to any area of conflict to begin with. The very nature of peacekeeping invariably calls for unpalatable actions to take place for the greater good. And only the blissfully ignorant would believe that very few secrets exist in any UN headquarters.

The bottom line is that Hammarskjöld's "clean hands" aspiration frequently resulted in bloodied peacekeepers and butchered civilians. While many UN personnel, both military and civilian, despaired of such international innocence, there was an even more farcical episode regarding the triviality accorded such an important military function.

O'Brien's memoir recalls:

We infringed the "clean hands" doctrine to the extent of employing in Elisabethville one Greek ex-policeman with an imperfect knowledge of French who was already—as we later found from captured documents—known at the headquarters of Tshombe's Gendarmerie by the proud title of "Chief of the United Nations Intelligence Services in Katanga."

The rest of the said services consisted of a few Baluba houseboys who, sometimes for money but more often out of sheer political zeal, would bring scraps of information, usually alarmist gossip, from time to time. This is what Col. Waern meant when he referred to "my spies."

O'Brien later rightly describes the intelligence gathering, particularly what intelligence professionals call "handling agents" or "running agents" (a generic term for someone managed by a professional intelligence officer and who gives information—similar to an informant) as having been "bound to become a little comic."

Frankly, it beggars belief that McKeown, much less O'Brien himself, was expected to operate a complex civil-military operation with such a set-up. Indeed, in the case of Niemba, studies later showed that a lack of tactical intelligence gathering contributed to the loss of the nine Irish soldiers.

In the case of Jadotville, the same thing can also be said. Both the strategic and tactical intelligence appreciation of the situation was sorely lacking.

However, for A Company and the rest of the Irish troops of the 35th Battalion, all these concerns were purely academic. The rank and file, as they made their arrival into the Congo, were blissfully unaware of the top-level shortcomings that were soon to endanger their lives.

5

DEPLOYMENT

All my bags are packed,
I'm ready to go,
I'm standin' here outside your door,
I hate to wake you up to say goodbye.

—JOHN DENVER,
"LEAVING, ON A JET PLANE"

For the boys of A Company, volunteering to serve in the Congo seemed like a great adventure. They were mostly in their late teens or twenties, with only a sprinkling of old soldiers.

John Gorman, not long turned seventeen, enlisted underage like so many of his comrades had done in those drab times, and to him the idea was thrilling.

"It wasn't that long ago in terms of time," he says,

but in terms of opportunity, it's a couple of lifetimes away—
especially when I think of the opportunities available to my

youngest daughter now and the rest of her generation and compare it to that period.

Youngsters today think nothing of jumping on a plane to go to Australia for a year. If you had the fare to jump on a plane in our day you were going for the long haul. For most of us the Army represented a chance for a secure living. For some it was a career and for others it was a chance to get some money together to get away.

When the Congo came along, it represented a huge change in the opportunities available to us both in the Army and in Ireland in general. It meant something for all, a chance for extra money, a chance to do some real soldiering, but most of all a chance for travel, adventure!

The troops of the 35ᵗʰ Battalion were drawn from all over the Army, and included B Company—the Southern Command, and C Company—the Curragh Command. Attached to the 35ᵗʰ Battalion was an Armoured Car Squadron comprised of Vickers 1945 vintage vehicles and an artillery battery of 120 mm heavy mortars.

The men of A Company were volunteers drawn from the Army's Western Command. This included troops from the garrisons in Athlone, Mullingar, Galway, and Finner Camp in Donegal. For many of the troops it is no exaggeration to say it was their first time outside their native counties.

Sgt. Walter Hegarty recalls that "many of the lads were expecting to see a country filled with giraffes, lions, and tigers. After all, we could only know what we had seen in the cinema—*Tarzan* films and the like. There were very few people living around Galway in those days who could give you an accurate description of Africa."

A Company formed up as a cohesive unit on May 30 to begin

training and preparation under their new CO, Comdt. Pat Quinlan. There was an air of expectancy and the sun was shining. The previous month, the Russians had sent a man to the moon. Apart from his military background, Major Yuri Gagarin didn't have much in common with the Irishmen drawn up on the square in Custume Barracks in Athlone that May day, except perhaps a blinding sense of enthusiasm.

The soldiers underwent the normal tedious routine of inoculations and were given a myriad of lectures warning them of the dangers of fraternizing with local women. The young troops were cautioned that African women "can be quite possessive."

The truth of the matter, however, was that the only information worth going on was that which was filtering back from those who served on the 33rd and 34th battalions. For most of these troops, the political reasons for their tour of duty were not as prominent in their minds as the knowledge that nine of their comrades had died trying to keep the peace at Niemba less than a year previously. Even so, like perhaps all young soldiers before them who have gone in harm's way, they were outwardly optimistic.

A letter from Pte. John Manning, later to be wounded at Jadotville, illustrates how many of the troops were thinking:

Custume Barracks, Athlone. June 1961

Dear Mickey,

Just a few lines hoping you're keeping okay. As for myself, I'm fine. Well I suppose you heard by now that I'm going to the Congo this Tuesday with the 35th Battalion.

I was down at home last week but I never got a chance to see you, I'll see you all when I come back at Christmas. I was very lucky to get going this time because I've only just passed out a few weeks ago and I was the only recruit that was picked out of our platoon to go.

There were four of us picked but the Commanding Officer stopped the other three. I had passed out as Best Soldier and I also got a prize for Best Kit. I got the certificate at home and the bit of paper with our names in them. The photograph with me shaking hands with the Colonel won't be in the paper till I'm gone to the Congo because they're also putting something about it in it.

Well we don't know what place we're going to yet but when I get there I'll send you a letter.

From, John

That June, while the troops were busy with preparations for departure, their wives, parents, girlfriends, and siblings quietly nursed worries for the trials that lay ahead for their loved ones.

Lt. Noel Carey remembers:

I was engaged to Angela O'Sullivan who was a theater nurse in the Mater Hospital in Dublin. On the Whit weekend we were due to go to Limerick and I had to break the sad news to her that I had been selected to go to the Congo in June as platoon commander of No. 3 Platoon, A Company, 35th Infantry Battalion, ONUC.

Naturally it was a shock for Angela, as we planned to get married in September and she was upset at the news. We discussed getting married prior to my leaving but decided against it as it would be unfair to Angela. She decided to continue with her job in Dublin while I was away.

Lt. Carey didn't realize it at the time but, instead of undergoing the rite of marriage that coming September, he had unknowingly substituted it for another time-honored rite, that of the baptism of fire.

Parting from family is always hard for the serviceman, but for the men of the 35th Battalion, the god of Peacekeeping decided to be a little more than perverse.

After everyone had said their goodbyes and soldiers had prized themselves from the tearstained arms of their families to go out to Baldonnel Aerodrome, they discovered that the flight had been canceled. And it was canceled again the following night.

For the local men, this was a chance for two more precious nights of wake with their families. For the younger midlands soldiers like John Gorman, however, it was a nuisance:

Most of us had said our goodbyes in Athlone. Some families had traveled up to Dublin, but with the nature of public transport and the cost, they were gone home that evening. We young lads were chomping [sic] at the bit to get going and finally get out there. For nearly all of us it would be the first time on a plane.

The bittersweet nature of what most of the troops were feeling as they prepared to board the giant USAF Globemaster aircraft can be summed by Lt. Carey's thoughts on departure day:

As I was passing the Mater Hospital the next morning at six a.m., I was thinking of my dear Angela going to work in the theater as we drove to the airport and a new adventure in Africa.

The troops embarked onto the Globemasters, each of which was big enough to hold sixty troops, an armored car, and numerous crates of the 35th Battalion's support weapons and equipment. On June 25, 1961, they finally got to see what the fuss was all about when they set foot in Elisabethville Airport, in the errant Congo province of Katanga.

As the 35th Battalion settled into Elisabethville, the situation was comparatively peaceful. A Company's first deployment was to a local factory on the outskirts of the city.

Despite the political calm, the early days were hard going as the troops adjusted to the new energy-sapping climate of very hot days that could reach a high of ninety degrees by midday, but would cool to chilly temperatures when the sun went down.

Comdt. Quinlan was an officer of the old school, who believed that the best way for his troops to acclimatize was to get straight into platoon drills for quelling riots. A physically arduous and draining type of military training at the best of times, this had the benefit of concentrating A Company on the realization that the luxury of a relaxed acclimatization was not for them.

As with all military establishments, a daily routine was established. Reveille was at 0700 hours, breakfast 0730 hours. Quinlan took his inspection at 0800 hours, after which training began immediately and continued until 1100 hours.

At this point a short break took place. Junior officers and NCOs recall that training was "relentless" and that Quinlan put them through their paces incessantly, all the time impressing on his subordinate officers that the training should be "as realistic as possible."

Lt. Noel Carey, only a young man of twenty-four on his first overseas operational posting, found the early regime grueling:

I fell foul of his tongue on many occasions, and he never seemed to be happy with my platoon drills, which caused much frustration, both to myself and my platoon, who were working very hard.

However, Quinlan, while working his men to their limits, was wise enough to realize they were largely untested, and he was obviously a believer in the old military adage, "More sweat on the training ground and less blood on the battlefield."

More importantly, the tough regime served to remind the troops they were now in a delicate theater of operations where the unexpected should be expected and prepared for as a matter of course. On a more prosaic level, such a physically full day took the men's attention away from other issues.

For example, the postal service to the Irish troops was abysmal. At times it took up to three weeks for letters from Ireland to reach the troops in the field. This was to be the cause of much worry and tension for the younger troops intent on keeping contact with their girlfriends back home.

The conditions at the factory were basic to say the least, with troops being billeted in outhouses and largely subsisting on pack rations. These were prepacked food boxes for troops on operations when there were no facilities for a field kitchen.

Nowadays, pack rations are issued on an individual basis to a soldier and he can end up with a choice between frankfurters and beans in a curry sauce or the old reliable Irish stew. When A Company deployed to the Congo, pack rations were generally issued on a section basis. That is, there was one much larger pack to approximately eight men, which meant a lot less opportunity for choice.

One of the staples in the pack ration of the time were large hard biscuits fortified with nutrients and universally known as "dog biscuits." The idea of the biscuit was that it was a simple, nutritious food item with a long lifespan, and so of good use to the soldier in the field with no access to hot food. It was quite tough but could be made edible by softening in water or using a spread. But it was not to all tastes, as Lt. Carey recalls, "I loathed the margarine and the dog biscuits which were dry and tasteless. We envied those at the Headquarters and I availed of any opportunity to go there for a decent meal."

Pte. John Gorman also recalled the ubiquitous dog biscuit:

> I remember them being as hard as bloody rocks. Some lads would steep them in water and eat them like a child with a rusk. Most of us would just spread this margarine—I think it was called Dolly Margarine—on them. The margarine was as thick as axle grease, but didn't seem to go off as easily as butter. I don't think any of us tasted real butter until we set foot back in Ireland. I suppose the margarine could be preserved easier in the African heat.

Despite the initial hardship, A Company soon settled into their routine, got used to the climate and to the food, and even managed to satisfy the CO's high standard in deployment and antiriot drills.

Football and athletics competitions were organized with other contingents, and the new Irish battalion competed feverishly, particularly against the Swedish, Indian, and Italian contingents. This was to be of some relevance, as it was troops from these contingents alongside whom Irish troops were later to find themselves fighting and dying.

Quinlan himself led the way in socializing with his fellow soldiers from the other contingents. Troops recall his convivial visits to the officers of other contingents and how they were often invited back to A Company's base.

Indeed, Lt. Carey remembers the night Quinlan and a Swedish officer ended up in a drinking contest following an intercontingent football match. However, despite the high jinks, which were no harm for morale, Quinlan continued to lead by example, "This did not stop Quinlan being up at first light next morning, as he was every morning, something I marveled at."

At this time, A Company was being subsumed into the military duties of the day, providing guards for UN positions around the city and its environs, as well as patrolling around the strategic parts of the region.

The most hazardous duty A Company had undertaken since their arrival in Africa was providing troops as guards on trains traveling north across the lawless borders between Katanga and the rest of the Congo.

After two months of this routine, A Company was rotated out of their billet, exchanging their area with B Company and moving on to the local airport. Later, the two companies would also rotate at Jadotville, with A Company taking up where B Company left off, but with much less good fortune.

A Company's new role at the airport involved patrolling the roads around this vital installation and assisting in unloading international aid from arriving aircraft. Despite this being what might be called a cushy number, Quinlan kept up his demanding tactical training program.

But then a chance came for a break from routine patrols and guard duty. Quinlan was detailed to send a platoon to patrol an area of Katanga adjacent to the Rhodesian border.

Lt. Carey, then chafing under his CO's Spartan training regime, jumped at the chance to get out from under the thumb and volunteered. For Carey and the young enlisted men, this mission seemed an opportunity for adventure like something out of a Kipling novel.

The platoon, approximately thirty-two men, were to be led by A Company's 2IC, Capt. Dermot Byrne. Their mission was to get to Dilolo, a village two hundred miles to the south, right on the Rhodesian border, to rescue a Congolese government minister and his family who were stranded there.

Such was the volatility at the time that this man would have been an instant target if he was recognized passing through Katangan territory. A convoy of two armored cars, two trucks, a minibus, and two jeeps was assembled, and the troops set off.

The initial leg of the journey was reasonably straightforward, as it was along a metal road to the very town that would later prove such a testing ground—Jadotville.

However, passing through the little mining town was uneventful and the metal road continued on to Kolwezi where the troops bivouacked overnight. Little did they know, the disused building they were bedding down in would be used to imprison them following capture at Jadotville just over a month later.

From Kolwezi on, the road deteriorated into a dirt track that wandered into the bush at times. As the little convoy wound its way along, the dirt and dust got so thick the troops all had to don goggles just to see in front of them.

Anyone who has ever traveled overland in Africa can testify to the unremitting jagged and ad hoc nature of the dirt roads. With deep drains cut in either side to cater for the monsoon rains, accidents are a way of life on these routes.

Sure enough, the Irish patrol soon came a cropper. As the convoy rounded a bend, the lead car careered off the road and into a deep ditch. Try as they might, the troops could not budge the vehicle.

Lt. Carey and his men eventually had to leave it where it was. After stripping it of its weapons and ammunition, they continued traveling deep into the bush until they came upon a mission school run by the White Fathers. Here they were able to rest up for the night.

This was to be the start of a catalog of equipment and transport problems that were to dog A Company and the Irish contingent in general during their tour of duty in the Congo.

The next day the patrol finally arrived on the outskirts of Dilolo. Along the way they were greeted by friendly locals working in the fields, who proffered bananas to the passing troops.

Nevertheless, when approaching the village itself, the troops were prepared for a less than welcoming reception. The main body of troops were deployed on the outskirts and Lt. Carey, Capt. Byrne, and their interpreter entered the village.

Despite some palpable tension in the air, the Irish managed to get the minister and his family aboard the minibus and immediately evacuated the area.

While the patrol proved largely uneventful from a tactical point of view, it was the first opportunity for the troops to see the real Africa and its people, and also to realize the shortcomings of some of the equipment they had taken with them from Ireland.

For Lt. Carey and the rest of the troops, the vegetation and countryside proved "fascinating, with fruits growing all alongside the roadway. In the bush we could see a group of baboons swinging in the trees. Along the road we saw sticks with pieces of paper attached. This was the local postal service."

When the troops attempted to return to base, incredibly, their transport was to let them down again:

> One of our trucks with the rations left the road. It took up to three hours to put it right, but the natives had by then removed a lot of our stores. Who could blame them? Luckily we had no one injured, but this delay meant that we couldn't reach our base by dusk, and we lingered on the road with an armed guard for the night. I slept fitfully beside the jeep and was fascinated to hear the native chanting coming from villages close by.

> I was awakened suddenly in the early hours with the sound of running feet and as I grabbed my Gustaf [submachine gun], I saw almost a hundred shadows pass on their ways to

God knows where. It was a chilling experience.

It should be remembered that this was a similar size body of troops to that which had suffered the massacre at Niemba. It was even more isolated from UN support and would have had recourse to only the barest intelligence reports telling them of the situation in the region.

On the return route, the patrol passed through a checkpoint manned by the Katangan gendarmerie and led by a white mercenary officer. After some tense discussions, the officer allowed the patrol on its way. But the Irish troops could sense the changing atmosphere as they returned to camp.

The patrol to Dilolo demonstrates how even minor tasks were magnified in their difficulty because of faulty transport and general unawareness of where large portions of the local population stood regarding UN forces.

Again, the soldier on the ground's job was being impeded by a lack of clear direction from UN Headquarters, and compounded by an Irish state that was sending men into harm's way with only the most basic of tools to complete their mission.

In an interesting footnote to Irish social history, the one part of the Irish contingent's structure that seemed to work seamlessly was the chaplaincy service.

Irish chaplains have a noble tradition of serving in the front lines, be it with the Irish regiments of the British Army in both World Wars or later with the Irish Army in the Congo.

Irish units have found them to be invaluable as a part of the structure in any overseas force, assisting with the men's welfare and morale and generally contributing to that most valuable asset of any military force, unit cohesion.

A Company had their own chaplain attached in the person of Fr. Thomas Fagan. Originally from Westmeath, Fr. Fagan was a constant figure to the troops of A Company.

Unlike other armies, chaplains in the Irish Army do not hold a commission—that is, they do not have an actual rank like captain or major. But they are generally regarded as of commissioned rank.

Theoretically, this unique position enables them to have the respect of officers and men alike, but still allows them to mix with the rank and file without the impediment of rank or social difference. Of course, as with most military situations, the efficacy of this idea tended to vary according to the caliber of the chaplain and his ability to earn respect and mingle easily with men of different educational and social backgrounds.

While Fr. Fagan was held in high regard by the troops during the battle at Jadotville, not all were happy at the exalted position the Army accorded to religious observances, as these comments from Lt. Carey following the Dilolo patrol show:

On our arrival, tired and disheveled as we were, the main concern was that as it was Sunday we must go to Mass. Reluctantly, I attended Mass with my men but resented the intrusion of religion as I did on a number of occasions subsequently. I felt that chaplains were allowed to interfere in military matters which were none of their business and were accorded too much authority and privilege in our Army of that time.

Others were to feel differently about the chaplain's role during active service, but Carey's comments perhaps simply reflect the beginnings of a change of attitude to the clergy's role in general in Irish society by a younger generation.

Carey and his platoon were not to have much time to recover from his first real eye-opening introduction to Africa. Following the Dilolo patrol, the operational tempo rose dramatically, and A

Company knew they had a game on their hands.

The posturing of the Katangan forces and the central role of the mercenary officers had become too much for the UN to take. This fact was to manifest itself directly on A Company's operational patch.

6

A RUM AFFAIR

I hear an army charging upon the land,
And the thunder of horses plunging foam about their knees:
Arrogant, in black armor, behind them stand,
Disdaining the reins, with fluttering whips, the charioteers.

—James Joyce,
"I Hear an Army"

Operation Rumpunch was the UN's direct response to the increasingly belligerent behavior of the gendarmerie, or gends, as the Irish troops had begun to call them.

The previously mentioned change of the UN resolution now mandated ONUC to a take a more forceful stance against the mercenary-led gendarmerie in order to collapse the Katangan secession.

As yet, a situation had not presented itself where the UN could apply this specifically. However, at midnight on August 26, 1961, an offensive move by gendarmerie troops into Elisabethville Airport, which was being secured by A Company, changed this.

A letter home from Pte. John Manning vividly illustrates the jump from the likes of the Dilolo patrol to the altogether more dramatic nature of events which followed:

Dear Mickey,

Just a few lines to let you know how things are around here. Well, I was on a patrol last week to rescue a minister's wife and children in Dilolo … (I just had to stop writing because gendarmerie soldiers are coming in to the airport. About two hundred soldiers are after trying to get in here and some got shot dead and I'm just after seeing a black's arm where he got stabbed by a bayonet. We're still on stand-to. We have an awful lot of prisoners here.)

Well anyway, when we came off the patrol we were told to take over the Gendarmerie HQ and capture all the Belgian officers. Well, we took over the barracks and captured all the officers and deported them to Belgium. I captured a few of them, one of them went for his revolver and tried to get away. We already got orders to shoot anyone that tried to escape and when your man tried it, I hit him an awful smack with the butt of my rifle and bayoneted him. He's lucky I didn't shoot him.

One of our officers saw me doing it and congratulated me on my action. There was a lot of shots fired and one Swedish interpreter got shot twice in the back. Later on that day, who came up to the barracks but President Tshombe, and me and a corporal caught him and disarmed his bodyguards.

We handed him over to officers and they let him go after a

while. Well, Mickey, that's all the news for now.

I suppose you'll read about it in the papers. Well, hoping to hear from you soon.

From, John

In his letter Pte. Manning encapsulates the events that subsumed A Company in the last days of August and the early days of September. His letter straddles the events of the gendarmerie trying to infiltrate the airport, the Irish response, and the execution of Operation Rumpunch.

Manning literally appears to have written the letter during quiet moments in between the action. His reference to having to stop writing "because gendarmerie soldiers are coming in to the airport" is a masterpiece of soldierly understatement. The gendarmerie was in fact moving in to occupy ground in preparation for an attack.

Comdt. Quinlan's report of the action states that on the night in question he had established mobile armored patrols based on his suspicions that members of the gendarmerie were in the area.

The armored patrols found nothing, but small, two-man listening posts sent out earlier and quietly secreted around the perimeter of the airport, alerted Quinlan to the fact that gendarmes were busy digging trenches in the vicinity.

The listening posts also reported that the gendarmerie were simply stopping work and taking cover at the sound of the patrolling armored vehicles.

As Quinlan puts it in his official report:

This was disquieting news as aircraft with Indian troops were due to commence landing at the airport very early next morning...I recommended to the Battalion OC that we should move in and dislodge this group at first light. At approximately 0230 hours I received orders from Lt. Col. McNamee [Battalion OC] that I was to take command of A and B Companies and move in and capture the gend positions at first light.

Essentially, Quinlan and his troops surrounded the gendarmerie force, putting in place a platoon backed with light machine guns to prevent the Katangans from escaping the trap they had led themselves into. A force of troops led by armored cars would move forward and take the Katangan positions after they had been called on to surrender.

The rest of the troops were to secure all roads leading to the Airport living quarters, thus stymieing any hope of reinforcements reaching the Katangan force. Quinlan stipulated to his subordinate commanders that fire was not to be opened except in self-defense. At 0600 hours the next morning, August 27, the Katangans, including two white mercenary officers, surrendered with a minimum of resistance.

As Quinlan had predicted, the force had been preparing to launch an attack that morning as the scheduled day's aircraft would have been making their landing approach.

If proof were needed, Quinlan had it in spades. The Katangans had sited two mortars on the runway with shell fused and ready to fire. Two light machine guns were also loaded and trained on the runway.

All of the personnel captured were armed with loaded assault rifles, most of which were automatic, of the FN type.

Quinlan even makes mention of capturing a radio set and operator which was in direct contact with the Katangan Headquarters in Elisabethville.

The following now demonstrates the sheer bloody-mindedness of UN thinking, within which the operational soldiers had to try and work.

Operation Rumpunch was scheduled to kick off the next day on August 28. Its objectives were effectively

1. to capture the strategic centers around the Elisabethville area,

2. to round up the white mercenary officers working for the Katangans and any other malign foreign influences and oversee their repatriation forthwith, and

3. to restore the UN's primacy as the leading authority in the region, both militarily and politically.

Despite these objectives having been decided upon and plans to put them into operation due to come to fruition in less than twenty-four hours, Quinlan was instructed to release most of the gendarmerie.

Incredibly, he was being asked to release men whom he and his troops would be coming to grips with again in the course of twenty-four hours. But this wasn't to be the only surreal move Quinlan was ordered to effect in the increasingly Alice-in-Wonderland landscape the UN was creating.

During the course of the airport operation, one of Quinlan's junior officers, the charismatic Lt. Joe Leech, had captured a Belgian officer trying to sneak in to the Katangan troops deployed at the airport. This officer turned out to be a Major Mathys, a senior Belgian gendarmerie officer, and listed as number one on the UN's list of officers to be rounded up in Rumpunch.

For unknown reasons, Quinlan was told by his ONUC superiors that he was to "release him…as his arrest at this stage might jeopardize Operation Rumpunch."

The same intelligence officer was not found again and managed to evade arrest in the subsequent operation.

This was not to be the last time the Irish, particularly A Company, were to find themselves expected to fight with one arm tied behind their back.

However, to understand these bizarre orders, one must understand that the troops were being directed by political masters intent not on winning a war, but rather effecting a peaceful solution and at the same time trying to remain nonpartisan.

This was proving exceedingly difficult with so many of the great powers blundering around Africa trying to implement their own agendas. There is no doubt that the powers of Europe did not cover themselves in glory during this period.

In the events which followed, many were only too ready to engage in attacks on ONUC in general and its Katangan leader, Conor Cruise O'Brien, in particular. Most of the attacks claimed the UN was overstepping its mandate and that O'Brien was acting in a high-handed manner. The truth was that the European powers were dismayed at their wealth falling into the hands of Congolese nationalists.

But if the Europeans, particularly the Belgians, were a manifest part of the UN's problem in Katanga, then the Russians were creating even more problems further north.

Another Congolese province, called Kasaï, had also attempted to secede from the Congo and the Russians had provided aircraft to fly ANC troops to the province to put down this insurrection.

Kasaï did not have the same wealth or the same wealthy European backers as Katanga, and so the Kasaï secession ended rather quickly, much to the UN's relief. However, the idea that the Russians had helped the ANC troops land there was like a red rag to a bull for the Katangan regime.

For O'Brien's administration, it made the prospect of enticing the Katangan leadership away from secession peacefully even more of an uphill struggle.

Unfortunately, the UN was really in its pioneering days and was trying to work out how to implement a rather grandiose strategy without recourse to essential tactical tools such as intelligence.

O'Brien notes that aside from the general objectives of Rumpunch, there were a couple of extra ones. One was the placing of Katanga's Minister of the Interior, the troublesome Godefroid Munongo, under house arrest for the duration of the operation. O'Brien states that this was so that he couldn't stir up tensions that might give rise to public order obstacles for UN forces prosecuting Operation Rumpunch.

For similar reasons, O'Brien ordered that the Post Office and radio station be taken over by the UN. As he himself stated, "It was clear that Munongo and the radio would be likely to whip up resistance and endanger the bloodless success of Rumpunch."

O'Brien also mentions that by denying access to the telephone exchange at the Post Office, Katangan leaders such as Munongo would not be able to contact or threaten anyone.

From the civil and political side of the ONUC house it is clear to see that Operation Rumpunch was designed to take the fuel from the fire. Extract the mercenaries from the equation and perhaps Tshombe, who, deprived of his warriors, would be more compliant in returning Katanga to the fold of the Congo.

From O'Brien's point of view, it was imperative that the operation be efficiently conducted so as to decrease the opportunity for confrontation. This is a laudable objective in its own right. However, as we shall see, in the desire to be magnanimous when the operation went according to plan, actions were taken that left the UN in a precarious position when fighting did break out.

Aside from the purely military reasons for Operation Rumpunch, there was also a psychological necessity for it.

The Katangans had been dropping leaflets around the Elisabethville area in the days preceding Operation Rumpunch trying to whip up an antipathy amongst the black population against the UN forces. The Katangan regime, backed as it was by white Belgian commercial interests, was keen to portray itself as an example of inter-racial harmony, coupled with black nationalism.

The idea was to convince the world in general and the black Katangan population in particular that the UN was the real bully here, and that the white-led gendarmerie were the ones to whom they owed their allegiance.

At 0400 on August 28, Operation Rumpunch began. As part of an Irish/Swedish/Indian force, A Company and their sister unit, B Company, were to play pivotal roles in the operation.

It was a stunning success.

In short, all objectives were taken with hardly a shot fired and no serious casualties on either side. A and B Companies managed to take 41 mercenary officers into custody. In all, 273 mercenaries were repatriated, very much taking the sting out of the Katangan gendarmerie tail.

A Company had the juiciest and probably most daunting mission of the lot—to take and disarm the gendarmerie HQ.

Lt. Carey recalls his apprehension as he and his men mounted Swedish armored personnel carriers that morning:

I had no opportunity to recce the area of operations and I had to brief my troops from a map of the area which was not really satisfactory.

Our immediate task was to disarm the sentries located outside the HQ and we expected that they could be a problem.

As Lt. Carey and his men were approaching the objective, other members of the unit were moving into position. CQMS Pat Neville and a detachment of men had positioned themselves by the back gate of the HQ.

Neville told his men not to smoke as they waited so they wouldn't give their positions away. "The lads were tense. It would be their first taste of action of any kind. I was nervous myself, but I couldn't let them see it. They were relying on me to appear calm."

By some bizarre sleight of hand and perhaps the natural cunning of a quartermaster sergeant, CQMS Neville had managed to acquire the keys to the back gate of the HQ. He was to effect a quick covert entry when he heard his comrades force their way in through the main gate.

As Lt. Carey and his men approached the gate in their Swedish vehicles, they made ready for resistance from the gend sentries—but to their pleasant surprise there were none to be seen. "To our great relief, we found them deserted, as they had fled on hearing our approach. We quickly set up a jeep with a Vickers machine gun at the road junction."

The task of crashing directly through the gates and the risks that went with it naturally went to Quinlan. At his side was the unit's senior NCO, C/S Jack Prendergast.

A battle-hardened soldier from Athlone, Prendergast managed the impossible task of seeming to be at Quinlan's side constantly and yet popping up beside young inexperienced soldiers just when they needed direction most. However, gentle encouragement was not in his creed.

As Pte. John Gorman remembers:

We were part of the assault platoon to accompany the CO and Prenders (the C/S) in the gate. Naturally we were feeling a little scared. I was only seventeen. I had lied about my age and had joined up a year earlier at sixteen.

But, even so, we were all itching to go. This was what we were here for. Quinlan looked at us after we had gotten into position. He checked his watch, nodded to Prenders, and said to us, "Right boys, I won't ask any man to do anything I wouldn't do myself. C/S, let's go."

With that he gave a signal, and a Swedish personnel carrier burst in the gates with Quinlan himself lepping [*sic*]over them on the trot. Prenders had just looked at us when the CO was running forward and hissed, "Move it." We did, we just got up and followed the pair of them, and by Jesus did we have to run to keep up with them.

They were a marvelous pair, a great officer and sergeant. Wonderful leaders. We trusted them completely. As long as we were with them we felt invincible.

After Lt. Carey and his troops had secured the approach to the HQ there was a sudden burst of gunfire.

"I took cover behind a wall, my heart pounding, not knowing who had fired and if we had casualties," says Lt. Carey.

Not an unusual act for a normal human being to take, especially a soldier not yet used to being on the receiving end of offensive fire. But he needn't have worried. The shots were part of a burst of submachine-gun fire from C/S Prendergast as he personally stormed the HQ's guard room.

The guard room is the center of security for any military base. It normally houses a party of armed troops who are supposed to be alert for a twenty-four-hour period. Posted sentries, when not patrolling, should normally be found with their weapons in the guard room ready for any eventuality.

For this particular Katangan guard detail, the sight of C/S

Prendergast charging their position and firing from the hip was too much, and they surrendered without firing a shot. Indeed, the C/S' shots were the only ones heard during the operation to take the HQ.

Meanwhile, as CQMS Neville and his party were making their way in through the rear gate they became aware of someone running. Then the company cook, a Pte. Smith, told CQMS Neville the man was coming towards them. As Neville remembers it, "Naturally we assumed it was a sentry and I made ready to fire. But the man called out. It was Lt. Joe Leech. He told us the lads at the front had just ran through like a dose of salts."

In fact, when C/S Prendergast had come upon the first Katangan sentry, the terrified soldier had immediately handed over his rifle and raised his hands. Within a matter of minutes, Quinlan and A Company swarmed through the HQ, surprising all they met. John Gorman and his other young comrades were busy securing the barracks when they came to a bolted door.

Gorman says:

One of the lads tried the door, a big heavy wooden door. All the rest had opened straight away, but this one was locked. In fact, it looked formidable. As we paused to decide the best way to deal with it, the C/S appeared out of nowhere and literally flew past us.

I remember him shouting, "That's how yez do it!" as he battered open the door with one boot and shoved his Gustaf in at a bunch of frightened-looking gends half out of their beds. Before we knew it he had them herded out the door and sitting outside with their hands on their heads. One man was detailed to watch them and the rest of us ran on after the C/S.

Out on the road, Lt. Carey and his men had their own episode of excitement when a car tried to speed past their road block. Both Lt. Carey and Cpl. John McAnaney, a Derry-born soldier and all-Army crack shot were on the point of letting the driver have it when the car halted.

The man claimed to be a civilian and said he hadn't seen the road-block. But, as Conor Cruise O'Brien was later to acknowledge, the success of Operation Rumpunch was tempered by the UN's lack of intelligence information. Many a mercenary simply slipped out of his uniform and, armed with false papers, was able to move with impunity.

However, the next vehicle up to Lt. Carey's checkpoint was driven by a mercenary officer with no such clandestine ambitions. As Carey approached the vehicle, he saw that the driver was an armed mercenary. He says:

I arrested the Belgian officer, who seemed to be making an effort to draw his revolver. We pushed him against the side of the vehicle, but it transpired that he wanted to hand over his holster and automatic pistol to me.

I took it as a souvenir and retained it until our later situation in Jadotville, where I hid it in the roof of the garage where we stayed. We later arrested an Air Force officer and a French mercenary officer, both of whom were handed over to UN police.

As with so many episodes of military service, this one too had a humorous side with an Irish slant.

It is said that no matter what part of the earth an Irishman goes to he will undoubtedly meet another. The men of A Company were to find a variation on this theme as they continued bursting in the doors of the barracks as they secured the gendarmerie HQ.

CQMS Neville and Lt. Leech had moved through the upper floors of the barracks where the quarters were reserved for senior European officers. They were largely empty.

The main action was over and the officer and NCO were in relaxed mood. Leech was revered by his men as an eccentric but efficient officer.

He carried a swagger stick, smoked a pipe, and exuded calm no matter what the situation. He looked like the stereotypical British officer of World War II.

"Look Q, there's one we missed," said Leech, nodding to a closed door and using the abbreviated title from Neville's rank to address him.

Sure enough, there was a door in the shade at the end of the corridor. It was shut and all the rest were open. Instinctively we felt something was up, and inched down the corridor.

There was a muffled noise from inside, like a little squeal a pig might make at market. Lt. Leech raised his machine gun and motioned for me to do the same. He looked the part all right—tall, handsome, and with his unlit pipe clenched between his teeth.

With a nod of his head for me to cover him, he suddenly kicked in the door and we dashed forward. We got a shock. Leech even dropped his pipe.

There in the bed was a Belgian captain and a gorgeous-looking young, blonde woman. As we came in the door she sat bolt upright … She was naked as far as we could see.

But before we could get over our shock, she let out a flood of swear words … in a broad Irish accent! It turned out she was a Cork girl working as an air hostess for one of the international airlines still flying into Elisabethville.

"You can go nowhere," mused Pat Neville, as he shook his head in recollection of the incident:

The pair seemed relieved and delighted after they got over their shock. They had wondered if it was a mutiny by the native troops.

Lt. Leech, having recovered his composure at this stage, announced, "We're not here to take you, Ma'am, but Captain, you are now our prisoner."

I remember the Belgian captain. He was an older man. He just laughed and replied to Leech, "You were a small child when I was last a prisoner," referring, I suppose, to World War II.

The operation was considered a resounding success by Conor Cruise O'Brien initially, because he believed that the Katangans would be less likely to engage in belligerent acts now that the UN had staged a show of strength and deprived them of their mercenaries.

But there were still problems to be ironed out. The Belgian government accepted that any officers on secondment could no longer be involved with the **gendarmerie** and undertook to order those rounded up to leave and return to Belgium.

However, many more of the Belgians were young enlisted soldiers, former paracommandos, now no longer under the diktat of the Belgian government. The Belgian Consul-General told O'Brien all his Government could do in this case was to "advise" these men to go home.

O'Brien was later to meet Comdt. Quinlan and his troops from A Company to congratulate them personally on a job well done on seizing their objectives without bloodshed.

"But when he was congratulating us, the UN were handing back the weapons we had seized, weapons we had turned against us when we arrived to Jadotville a few weeks later," remembers Pte. John Gorman.

So even though a large number of mercenary officers were flown out of the country, a large number of them had evaded the round-up.

O'Brien, in his book, *To Katanga and Back*, acknowledges that

> Rumpunch was only partially successful. It did get rid of a large number of foreign officers; by September 8th, according to the UN military returns, 273 "non-Congolese personnel in the Katanga Gendarmerie" had been repatriated and 65 were awaiting repatriation. That was a more significant contribution to the reunification of the Congo than anything the UN had previously done.

However, there were still 104 mercenaries unaccounted for—10 Belgian regular officers, 54 Belgian volunteers, 11 Frenchman, 4 Brits, 1 Pole, 1 Hungarian, 1 Dane, 2 Portuguese, 1 Swede, 8 Italians, 1 South African, 1 New Zealander, 4 Dutchmen, and 5 of undetermined nationality.

The UN had allowed the success gained by the soldiers who executed the operation to be frittered away by a combination of muddled strategic thinking and an inability to marry diplomatic and military objectivity successfully.

Now the exultant A Company would receive orders to deploy to Jadotville, ostensibly to protect the white settlers there from a massacre. But it would be these same settlers who would join with the mercenary-led forces in attacking them.

7

ROAD TO JADOTVILLE

Men jostle and climb to meet the bristling fire.
Lines of grey, muttering faces, masked with fear,
They leave their trenches, going over the top.

—SIEGFRIED SASSOON,
ATTACK

Following the success of their input into Operation Rumpunch,
A Company found themselves back at Elisabethville Airport
guarding the runway. It was comparatively light duty. One of the
more positive spin-offs was the fact that troops were the first to get
access to the British Airways flight that came via Johannesburg with
mail from Ireland.

The ordinary troops, while not privy to the political machinations
that were going on in the upper echelons of the UN, were nevertheless
well aware of a rise in tension between themselves and the Katangans.

As members of A Company wrote to friends and loved ones, a
common theme that cropped up in their correspondence was the
Katangan gendarmerie and their status.

Troops were keen to point out that these, their potential adversaries, were anything but similar in arms or training to the bow-and-arrow-toting Balubas that had been running riot in the imaginations of the ordinary Irish citizen since Niemba.

This letter of A Company rifleman Pte. John Manning illustrates how this rise in tension was perceived by the rank and file. It is also interesting to note that over the years things have changed little for the soldier on overseas duty.

The craving for news from home, however mundane, is a constant theme for the soldier on active service. Arrival of post is and always will be a major factor of morale for troops on active service.

Date: August 1961
No 811272 Pte. John Manning
A Coy 35th Bn, Irish Contingent ONUC
Elizabethville [*sic*], Congo
BPO BP 37 B.

Dear Mickey,

I received your last letter okay. I sent some postcards home and I forget now if I sent any to you. I had a letter from Mam and she sent me on the bit of the *Leitrim Observer*.

I bet that shook a lot of the people around Mohill. Here's a ten franc note. When you're taking a drink you can take out that and you'll see the country men the way they'll look at it.

Give one of these tens to Dad and tell him I sent it. The photograph on it is that of Tshombe. I suppose you often read about him in the paper. He's causing a lot of trouble here. Last night we were on a special alert because we were told that he was moving with his troops to North Katanga and that he might try to overtake the airport to get his troops out.

There was a big meeting in Léopoldville last week and he was told that if he didn't attend it, the United Nations wouldn't stop the Force Publique [that is, the ANC] coming to Katanga.

Well he didn't attend it and we're still standing by to see what his next move is. The people at home think we're fighting them, and them with only bows and arrows!

Well they're wrong because they're better equipped than the Irish Army!

They have all the latest weapons. I don't know where they get them from but if they start anything there's going to be a tough time trying to stop them. I hear some talk about Russia sending someone in here.

Have you read anything about it in the papers? You know at times out here it's just like at home, but a fellow has to be on his toes because trouble could start anytime.

They weren't expecting anything to start at the Niemba ambush but they soon found themselves wrong. Only the other day the UN shot a Tshombe soldier at Niemba.

Well Mickey, I haven't any more news at the moment. But let me know if you read anything in the papers about this place. Well, hoping to hear from you soon and see you all at Xmas and we'll have a good time when I go home.

From, John

A point of interest here is Pte. Manning's awareness of the gravity of any forthcoming action due to the difference of armament between UN and Katangan forces. Would that the UN's planning apparatus had been as prescient as the young soldiers.

The other interesting point, one that has been a constant for the infantry soldier down the ages, is the sheer lack of information afforded to troops who are soon to find themselves in the thick of it.

Following a relative static period at Elisabethville Airport, preliminary plans were made to deploy A Company to an area along the Angolan border to combat the smuggling of weapons across the border to the mercenaries.

Lt. Carey was among an advance party that was selected to go by helicopter to prepare the way. As deployments go, this one had all the ingredients of a sweetheart posting.

The company would have been based at a village called Matoto, right on the Angolan and Northern Rhodesian borders. Lt. Carey and the rest of the advance party were even allowed stroll across the border into Rhodesia, where they met some Irish nuns who insisted on showing the small party of troops the best of Rhodesian hospitality.

We had a fabulous meal and even Rhodesian cream butter. They planned to contact me when I arrived with my platoon and said that I could come across and they would bring me on a tour of the country. I was eagerly looking forward to my new mission.

But this was not to be. The orders to move to Matoto were canceled and the company received fresh orders that Sunday, September 3, 1961, to deploy to Jadotville, a small but prosperous mining town approximately eighty miles north of Elisabethville. Carey's recall for their new deployment is clear. "Our mission in Jadotville was to protect the civilian population. The request for this protection had come from [Paul-]Henri Spaak, the Belgian Foreign Minister."

There would be no Rhodesian cream butter there. The troops of A Company soon received orders to deploy to Jadotville, and the venture was fraught with difficulty from the start. On a practical level, the Company had only one unreliable truck, one saloon staff car, and two jeeps.

The bulk of transporting the 150-strong group was carried out using borrowed Swedish trucks. In addition to the troops, there were also stores, bedding, and weapons to be transported—no small logistical operation in any army.

But even with the borrowed vehicles, there still wasn't enough transport. The Swedish trucks could only take 120 troops on the first leg of the journey. A second journey had to be undertaken just to get the rest of the troops deployed.

A number of items normally essential for any troop formation were left behind. They included the unit's supply of ten-day emergency rations and the eighty-one mm mortars which an infantry company relies on for in-house artillery support.

Accompanying A Company were two World War II–era armored cars, armed with Vickers machine guns and detached to A Company under the command of Lt. Kevin Knightly.

This was all proving to be a leap into the unknown for the entire unit, and a hell of a jump from the kind of duties A Company had been carrying out until now.

While the troops were deploying, they had no real comprehension of the intricate web that was being weaved around Katanga at this time. This web was largely in the area of perception management and done very efficiently by the Katangans. It goes some way to explaining what people ask to this day. Why were troops sent to Jadotville and isolated from support from their parent unit?

Prior to Operation Rumpunch, the image the Katangan regime wanted to project to the world was that of a small, plucky state where black and white lived in harmony and prosperity, but was the victim of UN bullying.

It played down the notion of Belgian and European commercial patronage, and also attempted to portray the persecuted Baluba tribes as savages that needed harsh handling by the gendarmerie, because the UN were not up to it.

Following Rumpunch, the image-makers in the Katangan Information Ministry were busily changing tack again. Now the message going out to the world was "Yes, everything is great, but Rumpunch has destroyed that by limiting our ability to govern. Now the UN must guarantee the security of our people, black and white."

Now that the mercenaries were supposedly no longer in command, the illiterate Col. Muké, former Force Publique sergeant major, was put back in the limelight. His fealty to the Belgians was total. They had made him what he was and he would not forget this.

However, aside from being "their man," Muké also allowed the Belgian settlers to demonstrate to the world the limits of Africanization in Katanga. This also gave rise to what in retrospect seems like a well-orchestrated Belgian-led psychological operation.

In military parlance, Psychological Operations, or Psyops, are used to sway an enemy force or a civil population. Psyops mess with the way people see things, or to use the more formal term, they "manage perception."

While propaganda can be used as part of this, Psyops don't rely on it exclusively. They can encompass real events, cultural interpretation, and some military action, all molded towards one function—the manipulation of perception.

They can be used at the tactical level to influence battles, or at the strategic level to influence the conduct of a campaign or avert the need to commit troops at all, but still achieve objectives.

If used judiciously, they can enable a militarily weaker opponent to carry the day.

The UN had declined to use their Public Information cell to be an instrument for influence. Conor Cruise O'Brien even mentions how he received a rebuke from ONUC HQ in Léopoldville when his staff used broadcast facilities to try and influence native Katangan troops to arrest their white officers during a later operation.

Later we will see how this could have influenced a positive outcome at Jadotville and perhaps alleviated bloodshed. The other result of not conceiving and executing information operations of any kind was that the UN were largely powerless to react to false information and recognize when they were being spun a line.

With the benefit of hindsight, O'Brien recognizes this when he wrote about the identifiable change in mood following Rumpunch:

> The worst thing the UN had done, according to *La Libre Belgique* [a right-wing Belgian newspaper], was to break up "the beautiful friendship between black and white" which, up until then, had prevailed in Katanga…The remarks—which were to some extent echoed in parts of the British Press—about the UN's having broken the beautiful friendship between black and white struck us as being silly. In fact they were not silly at all. They covered—with the half-instinctive intelligence of the determined psychological warrior—the need to make a rapid transition from one propaganda line to another.

The new reality had been manufactured in Katanga and was now being eaten up by an eager international press corps. It was the image of a destabilized state with a white population who, now deprived of their military shield, were in imminent danger of being massacred by an angry and unrestrained native population.

This resulted in a number of actions both within the Congo and on the international stage which now seemed guaranteed to force the UN's hand.

First off, O'Brien was informed by the consuls representing Belgium, France, Britain, Italy, and Greece that if any calamity was suffered by their citizens in Katanga, they would hold the UN responsible.

The Belgian Consul even demanded to know what preparations the UN had made to protect the lives and property of foreigners in Elisabethville and its environs.

The honorable exception from this diplomatic ganging-up on the UN was the US representative, William C. Canup. The US had regarded the Europeans in general and the Belgians in particular with a jaundiced eye in their machinations over Katanga.

While the Belgian establishment in the Congo sought to put pressure on the UN now to protect the ordinary Katangan and European citizens, they also emphasized how the gendarmerie were denuded through Rumpunch. The Belgian government also put in place a campaign to severely hamper ONUC operations on the world stage.

As Lt. Carey correctly noted, when A Company received their initial instructions to move to Jadotville, it was on foot of a request by the Belgian Foreign Minister, Paul-Henri Spaak, made in no less august a forum than the UN assembly in New York.

Spaak was no mean politician. A man who stood at the helm of his country as premier in the postwar years and had previously served an earlier stint as Foreign Minister, he was more than capable of getting his way.

With his Churchillian features all atwitch with righteous

indignation, Spaak proceeded to inform the world through the prism of the UN assembly that Katanga now teetered on the edge of anarchy. He went on to paint a lurid picture of the massacres that would take place, not only of white settlers, but also of loyal native Katangans, because the UN were not attempting to deploy troops into isolated areas of Katanga.

However, all was not what it seemed. The world was being presented with an image of a cavalier UN force being led by a swashbuckling Irishman intent on destroying peace and stability, but in reality, the truth was busily being bent according to needs.

Ray Moloney, a wire-service journalist with United Press International, describes here what he believed were incidents contrived to influence international public opinion and discredit the UN:

> I watched the Katangan government mount a deliberate "hate campaign" against the UN. I saw UN troops being stoned even though they made no attempt to retaliate. The stoning attacks were led by officials of the Katanga Information Ministry while it claimed that UN Indian troops raped and pillaged their way through the African quarters of Elisabethville.

In short, following Rumpunch, a propaganda war had sprung into being and the UN were not winning it. To say this war came out of nowhere would be disingenuous. It had been bubbling away for some time.

But now it was coming into its own, as it completely stymied ONUC's ability to make accurate assessments and take proper tactical decisions. It was becoming extremely difficult for impartial journalists to get a clear picture, and in any event there were a fair number of partial journalists only too willing to showcase the UN's fumbling.

As O'Brien puts it, "What the UN said became—for reasons to be considered later—muffled and inconsistent; what the Katangan Government said was war propaganda of unbridled mendacity."

Katangan civilians, particularly the white variety, were consistently backing whatever line their Government ran with, no matter how untruthful. Coupled with this was the fact that many "eyewitness" reports to media were given by people with a heavy bias.

For example, O'Brien says:

The reader in England, or the United States or Ireland or Sweden, took the "eye-witness accounts" of these people at their face value. Statements of "X, a doctor," "Y, a priest," "Z, a Red Cross worker" sounded impartial and reliable, and were always heavily damaging to the United Nations.

What the reader did not realize was that all these people were fighting the United Nations—by word of mouth always, and often with weapons in their hands as well.

One thing the reader may ask, and continue to ask at other junctures in this book, is why didn't the UN make any clear attempt to counter this harmful misinformation with means of their own?

I propose that the answer to this can be found in the earlier references to their antipathy to establishing a proper intelligence-gathering and collation facility. Countering misinformation properly requires timely and accurate intelligence. Only with this can you influence the perception of the public and persuade them that your information is more accurate and believable.

What now seems a well-organized propaganda and psychological operation was later to be corroborated by no less a journal than the *Peacekeeper's Handbook*, a publication designed to enable peacekeepers on current missions to avoid the mistakes of the past.

The *Handbook* claims:

Information services have a role in creating the necessary emotive response, both inside and outside the country. Media can arouse emotions that can trigger national movements of action and reaction which can simultaneously or later be amplified by partisan sympathizers in other countries or political groupings.

Certainly the ONUC operation had lost any initiative in that regard to the Katangans. It goes on:

The Congo provides for many examples of where irresponsible and false information was generated to hinder UN peacemaking efforts. Mercenaries in the employ of Katanga formed an "information commando" to produce and publicize "atrocity stories." The stories, now considered to be false, enabled mercenaries to transmit and influence several world capitals. This was achieved with the assistance of a network of supporters and sympathizers. This network then fed the stories to media outlets and news agencies in these capitals where they were internationally disseminated. The UN was at a tactical disadvantage, because the stories had to be investigated and an attempt made to verify facts. Meanwhile, the mercenaries had made an international impact that affected the political and diplomatic status-quo.

This goes some way to explaining the potent effect of Mr. Spaak's rhetoric on his international audience. The Katangans were not solely relying on Spaak's eloquence to influence, but they were also putting their faith in the gathering momentum of press coverage of "atrocity" stories.

What could the UN have done? Well, the *Handbook* goes on to say:

> The only ways of countering this are to be able to respond rapidly with accurate info, graphically countering the opposition, or engage in preemptive propaganda operations. This is difficult for UN forces as they must operate within strict guidelines. Counter-photography is one method available. Having photographers and video cameramen record instances where UN troops are committed to combat. This enables allegations of atrocities to be rendered invalid, where such actions are being viewed as they happen around the world.

These facilities were not available to ONUC in 1961. And at any rate, worse was to come regarding the potency of Katangan/Belgian influence, and it all can be summed up with one word: Jadotville.

While the Jadotville siege is relevant to Ireland because it concerned the fortunes of 157 of her sons, the event was of major importance to a significant part of the ONUC operation in Katanga.

The call from Spaak was for UN troops to be deployed to more isolated areas such as Kolwezi and Jadotville to protect white settlers from being massacred. The argument was based on the mercenaries no longer being in situ to lead the Katangan forces and operate the more complex equipment.

Yet many of these repatriated mercenaries simply reentered Katanga by a myriad of methods across the porous borders that surrounded her. O'Brien himself makes reference to how support weapons such as armored cars and heavy machine guns were still the preserve of the better-trained mercenaries. Black soldiers were simply put sitting in the turrets and told "not to touch anything."

Indeed, one individual made a confidential report to O'Brien of

Rhodesian soldiers being spirited across the border to bolster up the gendarmerie.

The individual stated that native Katangan troops were told "not to fight during the daytime, but by night because they can have the full use of Rhodesian white soldiers. These, he said, were the ones who manned all heavy guns and armored cars."

Apparently there were also reports of large formations of regular white Rhodesian troops massed along the border with Katanga. The Rhodesian leader, Roy Welensky, had also been engaging in diplomatic saber-rattling, claiming not only that Rhodesia wouldn't stand for Katanga being forcibly returned to the Congo, but that the UK was in agreement with him on this matter.

While the UK had made their discomfort known about force being used to deal with Katanga, and indeed elements of the British media took great delight in portraying O'Brien as a swashbuckling mad Irishman intent on wreaking havoc in Africa, they never moved from support of the UN resolutions.

But the effect of the Rhodesian support, covert and otherwise, was to act as a fillip to the Katangan regime in their attempts to resist reintegration. If UN Headquarters in New York were paying any attention to the reports from their own staff in ONUC they would have seen a more direct threat to their objective of ending Katangan secession than the wild pronouncements of anarchy echoing around the world.

In fairness it may be understandable that UN HQ be concerned about massacres happening under their umbrella, but perhaps greater effort could have been made by ONUC staff to appraise them of realities on the ground.

Yet in the run-up to the deployment of A Company, there were a number of significant pieces of information overlooked by the UN command in Katanga.

Col. J. T. O'Neill, in an essay about Jadotville written some time after the event, mentions how a patrol he was a member of was "assailed with assorted missiles and verbal abuse" from locals in the Jadotville region long before troops were deployed there.

Lt. Carey mentions how on their return journey from Dilolo, they ran into a roadblock on the road through Jadotville, along with a substantial number of gendarmes dug in defensively under the command of a white mercenary officer.

Remember that during this patrol, the unreliability of some of the Irish transport and signal equipment came to the fore. These were things that were to become serious issues in the later deployment to Jadotville.

Col. O'Neill also makes mention of "a major roadblock at the Lufira bridge, approximately eighteen miles from Jadotville. Unlike most roads in the Congo, that between Elisabethville and Jadotville was metaled and straight. Traffic passing along the highway was open to attack from covered positions and clearly visible from the air."

To even the most militarily illiterate reader, it was obvious that Jadotville would be a difficult place to reach if under concentrated attack. One might also ask why it was a good idea to send troops there to protect the locals, if the UN seemed to be so unpopular with them.

It has already been established that the only tactical reason for A Company's deployment was the safeguarding of human life. It could perhaps be construed that Col. O'Neill's comments about suffering abuse, if it was from native elements, could be reason enough to deploy a force to protect the white population in the event of a breakdown of order.

This, of course, was what the Belgian and international press was claiming in support of Spaak's UN démarche. Despite the continued presence of white mercenaries and the Katangans' continued desire to build up their armed capability, the UN were taking seriously the threat of a breakdown in interracial relations in Katanga.

In doing so, it now becomes apparent that they took their eye off the tactical ball regarding operational requirements on the ground. According to O'Brien:

> The new image—White Colony threatened by Native Revolt—was much nearer the truth than the old Multiracial Paradise. A revolt by the gendarmerie, or part of the gendarmerie, with the support of the very large discontented elements in the mining towns, against the Tshombe regime was quite possible.

O'Brien's dilemma, and the UN's too, was that if interracial fighting did break out, then the whites would be in a precarious position. However, at this point, more anomalies show up.

First of all, a complete uprising in the gendarmerie was unlikely. O'Brien later admits that the assumption that one might be on the cards was "open to question."

A previous example of such an uprising had occurred in the Bas-Congo region in a force where the officers were all white. The gendarmerie at this stage was, in name at any rate, commanded by the native Katangan Col. Muké. There were also now a number of well-educated black officers spread throughout the force.

"However," as O'Brien says, "this was no time for quibbles."

He goes on to provide one of the real clues for some of the UN decisions later taken, stating that the Belgian Consul was "stressing that the UN would be held responsible for any incidents involving Europeans that occurred in Katanga."

And once again we were back to the old canard of demands for "the UN's plans for ensuring the security of foreign lives and property since the gendarmerie, by reason of UN action, might not be any longer in a position to guarantee such protection."

This constant carping at the UN to fill the supposed void of order created by the (supposed) repatriation of white mercenaries began to find its target. Even sober and seasoned international operators now began to let visions of massacre interfere with tactical planning on the ground.

When the Belgian representative in Katanga professed his doubts about the white settlers' safety in Jadotville, a combined Swedish-Irish infantry group was deployed. Entitled Group Mide after the Swedish Major who commanded it, the force comprised one Swedish company and B Company from the Irish contingent. Group Mide's primary objective had been the safe conveyance to Elisabethville of the families of persons arrested during Rumpunch.

This reasonably substantial force also conducted what are generally described in military parlance as "fly the flag" exercises— that is, patrolling and generally showing a presence. This was partially to reassure the civilian population and make them feel secure. It was also to convince the local gendarmerie units of the need for good and sensible cooperation with UN forces.

By now Group Mide had reported increased levels of hostility being demonstrated by the local white population against the UN troops. The infantry group was ordered back to Elisabethville on September 2, where, according to Col. J. T. O'Neill's account, Major Mide reported to his superiors that the "white population were not only not in danger, but distinctly hostile."

The following day, September 3, the two-company infantry group with superior transport and signal equipment was replaced by A Company. To this day the veterans of A Company feel they were patsies, dropped on purpose into a situation that everyone knew was untenable.

As John Gorman recalls: "At the time it didn't make any sense. Why would you send in 150 men less equipped to replace a unit of 300 men?"

To this day there is no military answer to that question. In fact, the military wisdom at the time concurred with what the then young

Pte. Gorman and his comrades were thinking. When Group Mide departed Jadotville, the Belgian Consul was busy again getting his international consular colleagues from other European countries to join him in putting pressure on the UN and O'Brien in particular to deploy troops.

In his memoir, *To Katanga and Back*, O'Brien states: "M. Créner [the Belgian Consul] indicated that there were other important centers of European population—for example Jadotville and Kolwezi—and they wanted to know, also, what the UN proposed to do to protect these."

Despite this psychological leverage being applied with diplomatic finesse, the UN military smelled a rat.

Brigadier K. A. S. Raja, the CO of the Indian 99ᵗʰ (Independent) Infantry Brigade Group, thus the senior UN military officer in Katanga, insisted that UN forces be permanently withdrawn following Major Mide's report.

Raja, correctly as it turned out, believed Jadotville to be untenable on military grounds. The perceived military wisdom would demand that no more troops or resources be poured into a precarious location where the people to be protected were demonstrably hostile. However, there was another sound military reason for not sending 150 men off on what at best can only be described as a wild goose chase. The ONUC leadership in Katanga were now busily planning another major operation to follow up on Rumpunch.

This was to become known as Operation Morthor. The name often gets confused with the term for an infantry support weapon called a mortar, but in this case the name came from its Indian planners: "morthor" is Hindi for "smash."

Morthor was an appropriately monikered operation, as it was conceived to stamp out Katanga's continued secession and restore order once and for all.

Even though negotiations were continuing between the UN and

Tshombe's regime, the barrage of Katangan/Belgian propaganda was resulting in attacks and violence on UN peacekeepers.

The massacres and instability long preached about were threatening to become a reality as far as the UN was concerned. As for O'Brien, the UN resolution of February 21 gave him the authority he needed to execute Operation Morthor.

Amongst other things, UN Resolution S/4741 prompted ONUC to "take immediately all appropriate measures to prevent the occurrence of civil war in the Congo."

The planning for Operation Morthor was well under way when A Company trundled out of Elisabethville en route to Jadotville. From a military point of view, this now seems, on so many levels, like an act of madness.

The senior UN military officer, Brigadier Raja, deemed there to be no operational reason for A Company to go to Jadotville. Even O'Brien concedes that there was no real reason for them to have been deployed and that "it was a decision taken at the top."

In other words, the UN in New York, under the direction of Secretary-General Hammarskjöld, ignored the reports from their people on the ground in Katanga.

They insisted that troops be deployed to show the UN taking action to counter perceived threats of massacre. In this situation it really was a case of the film *Wag the Dog* coming true, in which political spin-doctors manufacture a war in Albania to bolster a discredited US president's chances of election.

The atrocity stories and fears stirred and stoked by Katangan sympathizers and Belgian ministers such as Spaak had made the UN ignore the true picture unfolding in favor of a manufactured reality.

With the exit dust of the larger and better-equipped force barely settled, Comdt. Quinlan received verbal orders from Gen. Sean McKeown to proceed to Jadotville to protect the white population because of fears of a native uprising.

It is normal, to say the least, when deploying troops on a sensitive mission, to ensure the CO receives a detailed written operational order. Known as an OPORD, this is what the CO will refer to when making tactical decisions in absence of direction of higher authority. However, for Comdt. Quinlan, there was only an oral instruction.

As mentioned at the start of this chapter, things were far from perfect as regards the deployment of A Company. The reason for their deployment was muddled, complex, and, above all, political. They were poorly equipped from the start, and facing a badly-outlined task which had been beyond a previous larger force.

Still, the order was given and, in the finest traditions of the Irish soldier, the troops looked to their front, swung up their arms, and marched off to get on with the job.

This decision was to have devastating consequences for Operation Morthor, and for the men of A Company.

8

THE JADOTVILLE JACKS DIG IN

For where there are Irish there's memory undying,
And when we forget, it is Ireland no more!

—RUDYARD KIPLING,
"THE IRISH GUARDS"

Plop, plop. Pause. Plop, plop. Sgt. Hegarty knew that sound and what it meant. The shouts of, "Incoming!" rang out along the trench lines.

Hegarty dropped the water cans he was carrying and tumbled towards a fold in the ground. He was too far from his trench to take cover from the incoming mortar rounds.

It was day two of the battle, and Hegarty had experienced the Katangans' erratic mortar fire already.

Sure they land anywhere and everywhere, except where they aim 'em, he reassured himself as he counted the seconds between the "Plop!" of firing and the "Thump!" of the rounds landing.

"Crump!" He didn't so much hear it as absorb it.

Damned if the first one didn't land twenty yards away. While waiting for the second to land I nearly died with fright. I'd say I learned what fear is right there. Indescribable, but I remember trying to dig myself into the ground and my legs extended stiffly shaking behind me.

His ears still ringing, the twenty-nine-year-old Galwegian clawed the red African dirt. His face pressed into it, he could feel its coppery taste in his mouth as earth and man attempted to merge.

"Boom!"

Before his brain could articulate it, Hegarty felt the searing shock. There was no pain; it was just as if he had attempted to lie on a bed of nails like an Indian fakir at a circus. He felt only the shock of the shrapnel embedding into the soft flesh of his back and legs, and the knowledge, somewhere in the back of his mind, that two more rounds were still in the air.

"The second one landed only ten yards away from me, and a voice inside said, 'Wally, don't hang around for the next one.'"

Sgt. Walter Hegarty, Wally to his pals, was up off the ground like an Olympian from the starter blocks. His body was numb and his hearing muffled, but his adrenaline flowed and he ran on autopilot, oblivious to the shouts of his comrades to get down.

As he tumbled headlong into the first available trench, all that kept running through his head was a line from a popular hit that year, "Yeah, yeah, my heart's in a whirl," from Neil Sedaka's "Calendar Girl."

Funny what goes through your head when you've nearly been blown to pieces, he thought.

Only a fortnight previously, Hegarty had felt life was passing him by. Sitting in an office processing paper up in the comparative comfort of Léopoldville, life was as good as it got that year in the Congo.

A comfortable bed, even a fan in the office, and the hits of the day belting out on the radio beside him all only seemed to scratch at his frustration.

> *I love, I love, I love my calendar girl,*
> *Yeah, sweet calendar girl,*
> *I love, I love, I love my calendar girl,*
> *Each and every day of the year.*

"Yeah," mused the bespectacled NCO, "each and every bloody day of year goes by and I'm still stuck here in an office in Léo while the real work is going on in the Katanga."

The young Galwegian was supposed to be the platoon sergeant of No. 2 Platoon of A Company, 35th Irish Battalion. Yet here he was, stuck up in an office in Léopoldville.

The sergeant had what could only be considered a plum job—handy hours, lots of freedom, and the use of a vehicle to dash around Léopoldville during off-duty hours.

Most would be happy to sit out the tour of duty in such circumstances.

I was working up at the university area in Léopoldville in an Irish-administered camp with what was probably the only Irish naval officer in the Congo, Lieutenant Commander Brunicardi. It was a nice job with lots of time off and Bruni-cardi was a lovely man to work with, but I was really missing the lads. I'd come out to the Congo to soldier and here I was a glorified clerk.

It was sunny outside and the native labor force were all in good form. Neil Sedaka lilted away in a cheery manner that was really getting up Walter's nose.

> *(September) Light the candles at your Sweet Sixteen,*
> *(October) Romeo and Juliet on Halloween,*

(November) I'll give thanks that you belong to me,
(December) You're the present 'neath my Christmas tree.

"Bloody hell," he winced, glancing at the calendar as Sedaka's syrupy lyrics dripped all over him. "It's the first of September already. The whole damn Katanga thing will be over long before I get near it."

He already knew his company had been to the fore in Operation Rumpunch.

"Sure hadn't Conor Cruise O'Brien himself come out to congratulate the lads after?"

Hegarty had joined the 1ˢᵗ (Irish-speaking) Battalion in Galway in the mid-1950s to soldier and taste a bit of excitement.

Having suffered ill health in his teens, he was late getting into the Army by the standards of the day, enlisting at the age of twenty-two. Despite a studious appearance enhanced by his glasses, he reveled in the physicality of life in the Irish Army.

His abilities and natural intelligence did not go unnoticed by his superiors and fellow soldiers. Within a short time of enlisting, he was a sergeant, and now he was supposed to be the senior sergeant in his platoon, a platoon he should have been running at Rumpunch.

Damn it! he thought. His so-called "ability" was what had taken him to this bloody office and away from the action.

Then, amongst the pile of documents landing on his desk, his movement order back to A Company, now billeted by the airport in Elisabethville. Before a minute had passed, he had sprinted to his quarters and was grabbing his kit in a fever of excitement.

Belting past the office towards the Land Rover, laden with webbing and pack, Sedaka crooned longingly, even pleadingly, over his shoulder, "Yeah, yeah, my heart's in a whirl."

"So's mine, *a mhac*," grinned Walter as he gunned the engine and sped off to join his company, just in time to load up for Jadotville. Less than three weeks later, Hegarty was penning these lines to an Army pal back in Ireland:

As I write this I'm a prisoner in a hotel in Jadotville...with the memory of four days of truly active service to keep me happy. I hardly know where to start and I don't think the courage and strength of character of this company of young men can be told in a short letter. "We don't know what the folks at home think of us now, but I'm a proud man to have been here. I've seen young Regan [a private from Roscommon] stand up in his trench and of all things give the raspberry to the pilot who had just missed his position by a matter of feet. Young Ready, only one year out of Naas [the Army Apprentice School, of which new graduates would only be around seventeen-years-old], was hobbling about with a Gustaf—two days after a tracer round had gone clean through his left thigh and set fire to his equipment.

By this time Hegarty had sustained his own shrapnel wounds.

When A Company rolled into Jadotville earlier that month it certainly didn't seem like they were expected to fight a pitched battle. Experts after the fact were to criticize Comdt. Quinlan for poor siting of his company defenses.

But what is forgotten is the fact that the company was directed to UN-selected accommodation at the Purfina garage located on the outskirts of Jadotville. It was chosen for suitability to accommodate the troops rather than with a view to defending the area. Further indications that Irish Battalion HQ didn't expect any trouble was the lack of an attempt to resupply A Company with what they had to leave behind.

A military formation left without support weapons and emergency rations is akin to a boxer fighting with only one glove and no access to refreshment from his corner man between rounds.

This lack of essentials, coupled with the previously mentioned foreknowledge of resupply difficulties by road if hostilities broke out, meant the meager garrison of Jadotville had unwittingly been left to fend for itself.

Jadotville was always going to be a center of attraction to the Belgian expat community, such was its mineral wealth. In 1961, it was a thriving copper mining town and had a large community of native workers for the mines and white engineering staff as well as a well-heeled international merchant community.

Now called Likasi, it is classified as one of the more prosperous small cities in the Congo and, with a population of over 220,000, is a major industrial, mining, and transportation center. It also retains strong links to Belgium, with many of the white settlers having stayed on to live there.

Once A Company settled into this vibrant multiracial community, Comdt. Quinlan immediately attempted to allay any fears that he or his men were there for any other reason than to protect their already harmonious existence.

The Kerryman's first act was to visit the local dignitaries and show them due respect. When Quinlan told the local Burgomeister that his troops would be at his disposal should any trouble occur, the official replied that Quinlan was not at all welcome in Jadotville.

Furthermore, Quinlan was informed that neither his men nor any UN personnel were welcome in the town. Before leaving town for his camp, the Irish officer made the prescient move of buying a large quantity of goods from a local German merchant for A Company's upkeep.

It didn't take an intelligence specialist to figure out that opportunities to continue to equip his company with provisions from local merchants would soon be blocked.

With a large chunk of his men's rations sitting in the battalion stores in Elisabethville, Quinlan's forethought significantly helped to enable his company to conduct any sort of later defense.

However, there was a less fortunate occurrence for the German merchant who sold him the goods. The local authorities clapped him in jail. For Pte. John Gorman, it was a surprise to see his CO stumping up to buy goods:

> I remember him returning with what seemed like half the shop. We couldn't understand it at first. Then we saw [CQMS Pat] Neville and his storemen grabbing the stuff and getting it put away. Sure this was the only way we'd have been fed.

On his return to where A Company were encamped, Quinlan immediately called his officers and senior NCOs together to inform them of the situation, and then radioed through a situation report to Irish Battalion HQ.

The continuing instructions to Quinlan and his men from higher authority were to persist in flying the flag in the region and demonstrate a UN presence, even though it was clear this presence was being considered provocative.

Nevertheless, a regular routine was established by the Irish troops in order to settle into their new environment and show to all and sundry that they were not in Jadotville in a coercive capacity.

The company initially were billeted in a series of offices and villas built around the Purfina garage. According to Lt. Joe Leech, commander of No. 1 Platoon, this comprised

> a single-story villa and out offices. Civilians occupied the houses on both sides of these buildings and directly across the road was a vacant space, one unoccupied villa with an overgrown garden. Behind the billets was a mixed bush and elephant grass area; slog on for some five hundred meters to a dry stream bed at the bottom of the valley.

Despite attempts by the troops to burn the grass, ideal cover for encroaching infantry, it failed to provide the necessary clearance. Lt. Leech's accurate post-action report gives some indication of the difficulties of trying to defend in battle a location chosen by UN civilian personnel with no thought to defense, as opposed to purely accommodation considerations.

As Col. J. T. O'Neill asserts, "company officers insist that they were given no choice in the matter but directed there."

Quinlan later had to endure the criticism of Indian Major Gen. Indar Jit Rikhye, the former Military Adviser to UN Secretary-General of the time, Dag Hammarskjöld.

Rikhye, in his book *UN Peacekeeping and the Congo Crisis*, unfairly cites Quinlan as the force behind the Irish deployment at Purfina.

He states, "Quinlan had camped there for convenience and for quick access to the European quarter, in doing so he had ignored tactical considerations. The invitation was obviously a ruse to entrap UN troops."

Obviously taking no account that Quinlan was simply following laid down instructions, as mentioned earlier, Rikhye conveniently ignores a couple of relevant points. The most obvious is that this was the same area Group Mide had previously been ordered to occupy.

The fact that it was near the European quarter bears out what Quinlan's verbal orders were—to protect the white population from massacre or atrocities.

Secondly, if it was such an obvious "ruse to entrap UN troops," then surely it was up to higher authority, armed with the accurate situation reports A Company were sending back to HQ, to direct any decisions about deployment.

In any event, it is interesting to note that Gen. Rikhye agreed in November 1961 that it was "urgently necessary to establish an efficient intelligence service which is totally lacking at the moment."

He made these comments in a Canadian paper for international peacekeeping entitled *Intelligence and Peacekeeping: The UN Operation in the Congo 1960–64*. The paper, in explaining the ad-hoc structure of intelligence gathering available to ONUC, demonstrates how this hampered all military operations during the ONUC mission.

Therefore it could only be described as churlish to apportion blame to a mid-level company-grade officer for what was in effect a failure of strategic and tactical intelligence gathering and analysis at both battalion and force HQ level.

As always with A Company, training continued over the coming week. For Lt. Carey, it was a case of more of the same.

"We were put back to antiriot drills and training and continued to go into Jadotville to show a UN presence. We continued to receive supplies and rations from Elisabethville."

However, reports were coming into the Irish company that unrest was being cultivated in the nearby mining villages and that white mercenary officers were agitating amongst the natives and stirring up dissent against the UN presence.

At this point, had ONUC HQ in Katanga developed an organized organic intelligence-gathering facility, this information would have had more impact. Had they a more developed defense against the disinformation being propagated by the likes of these mercenary officers, they might have even stymied the forthcoming assault on A Company.

Bereft of any of these force multipliers, Quinlan simply did everything any prudent commander could do. Even though higher authority gave him no warning of the impending Operation Morthor, much less any warnings of a significant threat to his own area, he opted to prepare for battle.

Though insisting that his men prepare defensive positions, Quinlan decided not to be too overt with these preparations so as not to appear provocative to the local gendarmerie units.

However, two days after arrival on September 5, the Katangans started to blockade A Company and prevent resupply by road from Elisabethville by deploying a heavily-manned checkpoint at Lufira Bridge.

Lufira Bridge, some twenty miles from Jadotville, controlled access to the town from Elisabethville. Whoever controlled access at Lufira would ultimately be able to control the battle.

Quinlan could see what was coming. He then gave one of the more significant orders of his career. He told his men to start digging. CQMS Pat Neville put it like this:

> Our CO, Comdt. Pat Quinlan, had all of our personnel paraded for what he described as a chat. He ordered everyone in the camp to have a trench dug by evening. It happened and everyone had suitable accommodation by dark.

This order, timely as it was, undoubtedly saved lives in the bombardments and air attacks that were to follow, although not everyone was in a trench during the attacks.

Apart from the unfortunate (or fortunate, depending on your viewpoint) Sgt. Hegarty, who was caught in the open and peppered with shrapnel, CQMS Neville was to spend most of the battle manning his store above ground, disbursing welfare and ammunition to his men.

Despite the obvious rise in tension, Quinlan was keen to keep things as normal as possible—hence the opportunity for the irrepressible Lt. Joe Leech managing to source a nearby private pool and to wangle an opportunity for his troops to use it.

He managed to drag Lt. Carey away from his duties so the two officers could take a dip. However, Lt. Carey bore the brunt of his CO's wrath on return and was put to work checking the radio communications.

A Coy troops preparing their trench positions before battles

Members of A Company, including CQMS Pat Neville, Capt. Liam Connelly
(both center), and Gnr. Billy Keane (extreme right, seated)

CQMS Pat Neville (seated in cockpit) and Cpl. Bobbie Allen with the damaged helicopter they both risked their lives to guide in to land

Comdt. Pat Quinlan, commanding officer of A Company, 35th Infantry Battalion, and Company Sergeant Jack Prendergast, the senior NCO of the company

Members of A Company with John Gorman (extreme right, seated) in Custume Barracks before departure for the Congo

Sgt. F. Gilsenan holding the A Company pennant as the unit formed up prior to their Congo departure

Members of A Coy making a river crossing prior to occupying the Jadotiville area. In the center is Pte. John Gorman. In the foreground, with UN peaked cap and shorts, is Sgt. Harry Dixon, the medical NCO

L–R: Command group for A Company: Comdt. Pat Quinlan, C/S Jack Prendergast, and Second-in-Command Capt. Liam Byrne

Sgt. Walter Hegarty DSM (with glasses) overseeing preparation of trench defenses

Lt. Noel Carey (center with white scarf) and members of his platoon with the damaged helicopter during the ceasefire following the battle

Quartermaster's storemen brew up tea as they settle into Jadotville some days before the siege

Member of A Company with some of the local workers in the Jadotville area before relations deteriorated

Members of A Company immediately after hostilities had ceased. L–R: Sgt. Tommy Kelly, Gnr. Billy Heffernan, Pte. Jimmy McCourt, CQMS Pat Neville, C/S Capt. Liam Donnelly, Dominic Harkins, Pte. Mick Smith, Sgt. Geoff Cuffe, Capt. Dermot Byrne, and Pte. Paddy Donnelly

Setting up the quartermaster's stores after arrival to Jadotville. At back: Gnr. Billy Keane (stores assistant) and Company Quartermaster Sergeant Pat Neville, plus two unidentified riflemen

Unknown officer, but possibly Dr. Joe Clune, the unit medical officer, with local child before Jadotville deployment

Company Sergeant Jack Prendergast in foreground talking to unidentified Sgt. during A Company's deployment en route to Jadotville

Commandant Pat Quinlan addresses a crowd of well-wishers following his troop's return to the garrison at Athlone, Ireland. The child in the background to his left is his son, Pat Jr.

L–R: Capt. Kevin McCarthy, local attached interpreter and Comdt. Pat Quinlan in the lead up to Operation Rumpunch prior to Jadotville

A Company command group before deployment to the Congo. L–R: At back: Capt. Kevin McCarthy, officer with face obscured (possibly Lt. Noel Carey), Lt. Joe Leech, Capt. Liam Donnelly, Lt. Tom Quinlan DSM, obscured officer (most likely Capt. Tom McGuinn). At front: Company Quartermaster Sergeant Pat Neville, Comdt. Pat Quinlan, Capt. Dermot Byrne (second-in-command), and Company Sergeant Jack Prendergast

19. APPRECIATION

The following is one letter of appreciation - there are other - written by Brig RAJA, OC KATANGA Comd on the departure of 35 Bn from the Congo.

CONFIDENTIAL

No 1004/7/GS
HQ Katanga Command
Elisabethville.

To:

2 December, 1961.

The Force Commander,
ONUC
LEOPOLDVILLE

Subject: APPRECIATION OF SERVICE - 35th IRISH BATTALION

On the departure of 35th IRISH Battalion from KATANGA Command I feel I would be failing in my duty if I did not express my appreciation as well as that of my staff and troops in KATANGA, of the fine work done by this very fine battalion.

2 The 35th IRISH Battalion has shown remarkable steadfastness and fortitude during the very difficult times that they have had to pass through during their stay in SOUTH KATANGA. They have been a fine example of restraint coupled with soldierly qualities in keeping with the highest traditions of the United Nations.

3 I feel that the fine example given by this battalion was in a very large measure due to the personal example, drive and soldierly qualities of Lieut Colonel McNAMEE, their commanding officer. Colonel Mc NAMEE has impressed me as being a fine gentleman with high soldierly qualities and possessing strong convictions and belief in the cause of the United Nations, which he has done his very best to uphold. This I feel contributed in no small way to the fine performance of this battalion during their six-months stay here.

4 I should like to make particular mention of Comdt QUINLAN, who was in command of the company that had the misfortune to suffer so much at JADOTVILLE. This officer needs little commendation as his performance in maintaining the discipline and high morale of his men during a particularly difficult stage of KATANGA Operations speaks for itself. I have great personal admiration for the initiative, courage, drive and restraint of this officer and I believe that he could be held as an example for all soldiers.

5 I am sorry to loose the 35th IRISH Battalion from my command, but I can draw satisfaction from the knowledge that they shall be replaced by another IRISH Battalion, which I am convinced will in every way live up to the standard created by their predecessors.

6 I trust that my feelings expressed in this letter will be conveyed to the appropriate authorities.

(Signed) KAS Raja BRIGADIER

COMMANDER, KATANGA COMMAND.

(K A S RAJA).

NOO
The Commanding Officer
35th IRISH Battalion ELISABETHVILLE.

Letter from General K. A. S Raja, Indian commanding general, commending Comdt. Quinlan and his men for their bravery and professionalism following their stand at Jadotville

Members of the crew of a Gustaf antitank rocket launcher
"standing-to" prior to possible attack

Unidentified officer during a patrol prior to Jadotville through the local village area

A Company personnel during church service (RC mass) prior to Jadotville

Cluster of the command group officers and NCOs during an "O" Group, or Orders Group, from their commanding officer, Comdt. Quinlan, during the Jadotville siege. Quinlan is in the middle on his knees; immediately to his left, as always, is C/S Prendergast (with cap back to front)

Post-hostilities, Lt. Noel Carey (with white scarf) and some of the men he commanded of No. 3 Rifle Platoon in front of the damaged helicopter that had attempted to resupply them with water

Members of A Company practice their public order drill relentlessly prior to deployment on Operation Rumpunch

Pte. Michael O'Sullivan at a firing position near Company HQ at Jadotville

CQMS Pat Neville in the process of rearming the company post-Jadotville and prior to the Battle of the Tunnel

Unidentified Swedish officer attached to the Irish 35th Battalion prior to the failed rescue attempt for A Company at Lufira Bridge

To Quinlan's chagrin, Carey had to report that the radios could not be relied on for interplatoon communications. True to form for a lot of Irish equipment of the day, the radios refused to work when the troops needed them the most.

They were old eighty-eight sets which were obsolete at this stage, and the batteries were awkward and defective. The sets were supposed to work up to ranges of half a mile, but this depended on good atmospherics. The most successful attempts at communication tended to be at night.

Communication with Battalion HQ was by means of a C12 radio set which, as Lt. Carey recalls, was "on the limit of its range… We also had a limited number of batteries but the signals detachment performed miracles in keeping communications open."

A Company also had telephone access between the villas and their HQ, but this was soon cut in the prelude to the battle. Certainly, Carey's comment about the efficacy of the signal staff was borne out throughout the Congo operation.

Both by using the Irish language to preserve communication integrity and exposing themselves in order to enhance the radio range, Irish signalers operated well beyond the call of duty. One story, location unknown, tells of a signaler who sat up a tree with his set in the midst of battle in order for his unit to retain communications with HQ.

In addition to the trenches being sited and dug, Quinlan instructed his officers to prepare a defensive plan and to site the sixty mm mortars, antitank guns, and light machine guns.

All the while, planning for Operation Morthor was taking place at ONUC HQ and all the while, A Company were kept in blissful ignorance of this.

This excerpt from the 35th Battalion's log shows that the tension was in the air:

Sept. 5: a mob four hundred to five hundred gathered outside the UN HQ and UN Hospital. Stones thrown and insults shouted.

Sept. 6–9: personnel injured by stones including CQMS Hamill, Armoured Car Group. A platoon was also stoned by mob—two casualties.

Sept 9: Gen. activity in Elisabethville increases, roadblocking occurs. UN transport destroyed.

By September 9, Jadotville had been surrounded by gendarmerie units who had set up roadblocks on all the approaches into the mining town. Quinlan dutifully reported this fact to higher authority.

As a result of this development, a platoon-strength patrol was deployed to Jadotville, but was stopped on Lufira bridge by a gendarmerie roadblock.

Compounding problems for the Irish Battalion HQ was the start of a refugee problem on their doorstep. This commenced on September 3, the same day A Company left for Jadotville.

The refugee camp was situated very close to 35th Battalion HQ and included forty thousand refugees. Thus the Irish Battalion was given the task of sorting out the myriad of water sanitation and feeding problems.

Further details from the battalion history reveal that all the whites in Jadotville had armed themselves against the UN. A Company could not now draw rations from traders as the town had been blockaded. They were now completely surrounded by Katangan forces:

Sept. 11: Reports that arms and knives have been issued to Africans in Jville. Indications of an attack being planned.

O'Brien took up the matter with the gendarmerie leader Col. Muké. A Company was then instructed to hold out as long as possible without resorting to force. O'Brien telegraphed his superiors in Léopoldville, "Gradually losing initiative, if it has not already been lost. Require clear directions as to line of action."

At a diplomatic level, O'Brien protested to President Tshombe that Col. Muké had agreed to withdraw all the roadblocks, but had failed to do so. Tshombe demanded occupation of Elisabethville Airport as a quid pro quo. O'Brien refused. A message from A Company on the same day stated that twenty whites in Jadotville were organizing natives to take action against the UN.

At 1815 hours, Col. Muké promised that the roadblocks around Jadotville would be lifted. O'Brien now believed that since the whites in Jadotville had shown they were definitely taking up arms against the UN, A Company would probably be withdrawn.

Later that evening, at 1915 hours, A Company sent a terse message: "Alert high here, situation v. dangerous."

The next day, September 12, at 0500 hours, a radio message from A Company stated, "Situation quiet."

The next morning a conference was arranged between Quinlan and the Burgomeister of Jadotville.

That afternoon, a party with rations for Jadotville was stopped four miles out and forced to return. At this stage, key points in Elisabethville were occupied by the UN: the Post Office and Radio Katanga.

That evening at 2000 hours, orders were issued for Operation Morthor. It began the very next day, and so did the assault on Jadotville.

9

THE LINES OF BATTLE

If your officer's dead and the sergeants look white,
Remember it's ruin to run from a fight:
So take open order, lie down, and sit tight,
And wait for support like a soldier.

—RUDYARD KIPLING,
"THE YOUNG BRITISH SOLDIER"

The noose was now tightening around A Company, and well the troops knew it. The Katangans could be heard digging into fortified positions around the general area of Purfina garage.

In the days preceding September 13, the sounds and sights of support weapons such as mortars and machine guns being driven into place were plain to see.

The Irish were now dug-in in classic company-in-defense positions with their backs to Jadotville, the town they had been ordered to defend. Their direction towards Lufira bridge and Elisabethville now was totally blocked. Traffic was only being allowed through at the whim of the mercenary OC.

The situation was now tense, to say the least. Quinlan was acutely aware that the Katangan forces had modern automatic rifles and access to eighty-one mm mortar support and unlimited provisions.

While the A Company riflemen were still only armed with the new automatic FN rifles, they still only had a small detachment of sixty mm mortars. Still, he mused, "at least I have the armored cars with the Vickers mounted machine guns. They'll make a dent in any attacking infantry."

However, his orders were still to avoid firing on the Katangans if at all possible, and to prevent any acts that could be construed as aggressive by the gendarmerie. It was a tall order given the atmosphere.

Compounding the problem of food only getting through intermittently was the fact that the water supply to the garage area was controlled from Jadotville and, as Quinlan was only too well aware, could be stemmed at any time.

In view of this, he gave CQMS Pat Neville his orders:

Two days or so before the battle got under way, Comdt. Quinlan let out a roar for me. He was always shouting for the Quartermaster like there was no tomorrow, but that was just his way. We got on very well and would always speak frankly to one another. There was a healthy respect.

Anyway, on this particular evening, when I went to see him, he had a visitor. He was an Irishman whose name was Kearney. I think he was a technician of some sort with Union Minière. He told Quinlan, "You will be attacked any day now."

Quinlan seemed genuinely surprised, for I don't think he thought the gends would be that quick to attack. When the man had left, I remember saying to him, "He's tipping you off." He said, "I know," and then he ordered me to have the men fill every possible container with water.

The man who came to see Quinlan and warn him of attack was Charles Kearney from Wexford.

He had been assisted by Terry Barbour from Belfast and Hamish Mathieson from Scotland. The three men were working as civilian technicians in the Jadotville area at the time.

These men, Kearney in particular, passed on vital information to both Quinlan and the Irish battalion at no small risk to their own safety. They later managed to gain refuge with UN forces at Elisabethville.

Lt. Noel Carey remembers the type of phony war that was occurring over those days as the Katangan mercenary-led force tried to spook the Irish:

On Saturday morning, the situation became even more serious when we were told that a truck had been stopped at the Lufira bridge and sent back to Elisabethville by Katangan troops.

I was ordered to go into Jadotville that evening and report back on the situation. I drove as far as the railway gates with two NCOs and a driver to find the gates closed to us. I dismounted and walked as far as the gates which were at the entrance to the town.

I saw a number of Katangan armed soldiers and a white mercenary officer, to whom I spoke. He informed me that the UN would not be permitted into the town... This information was relayed to our Battalion HQ. The situation deteriorated further on Sunday, when we were alerted by sentries manning the trenches who observed soldiers moving towards our positions through the bush.

At this point the Katangans had begun moving in large numbers of troops culminating in a brigade-strength unit of approximately three thousand or more men. These troops were commanded by mercenary officers, a mixture of French and Belgians.

The ordinary Katangan gendarmerie was augmented by younger European mercenaries of junior NCO rank. These were largely young Belgians who had completed national service in the paracommandos and were either looking for adventure or had family ties to Katanga.

At this point there were also a number of former French Foreign Legionnaires mixed with Rhodesian and South African adventurers sprinkled throughout the gendarmerie.

In any event, the presence of these skilled soldiers meant that the mercenary officers could plan attacks with recourse to the full panoply of support weapons. It requires experienced and skilled soldiers to operate mortars and light machine guns in what is termed the sustained-fire role.

Without getting too technical, the support weapons enable an infantry force to inflict damage on an enemy without having to get too close. In other words, a good mortar man or machine gunner can lay down fire on positions from quite a distance off, so allowing the foot soldiers to get closer and closer without being engaged by the defenders.

The gendarmerie OC was named Michel de Clary, a vagabond French soldier of fortune who had extensive experience of fighting in France's former colonies.

It is also believed that the notorious Comdt. Falques, having fought in Vietnam and survived their prison camps, was now directing all mercenary-led operations in coordination with the Katangan reaction to Operation Morthor.

The odds were stacked against Quinlan. Ranged against him was an extensive, well-armed, and well-led force. The intelligence that the UN had garnered about "the blacks not fighting" was negated by the number of paracommandos littered through the force to stiffen their resolve.

These troops, distinguishable in their camouflage fatigues, were daring and courageous, and fought with the élan of the airborne soldier worldwide.

As Lt. Carey has mentioned, the Katangans had now started holding exercises quite close to the Irish lines. This was really a ploy to probe the Irish outer defenses and to test their reaction time as A Company were called to "stand to" every time the Katangans came too close.

It was also a form of Psyops (or Psychological Operations), as the mercenaries' favorite form of attack was to drive straight at a position in a machine-gun-laden Land Rover blazing away merrily.

The mercenaries had used this to great effect, terrorizing the Balubas in previous attacks. Now they regularly buzzed Irish lines, training their weapons on the Irish trenches, but stopping short of opening fire.

This was an extremely tense time for Quinlan and the rest of A Company. All it would have taken is for one nervous young trooper to squeeze off a shot and all hell would break loose, with the Irish being blamed for commencing hostilities.

In any normal theater of war, such acts as those of the Katangans would have been enough to justify a reaction from defending troops. It could rightly be claimed that every day of probes by the Katangans was extra intelligence for their attack.

Yet Quinlan held to his orders of not opening fire unless "absolutely necessary." The real accolades here, however, have to go to the junior officers and NCOs who managed to keep their young charges in check when at times it must have seemed like madness not to open up on the marauding Land Rovers.

But for Pte. John Gorman, it wasn't as bad as it seemed:

We were very nervous, but nobody could say we were frightened. Maybe excited, but not frightened. You see, we had great leadership, especially with the NCOs on the ground. Prenders was great [C/S Jack Prendergast]. He was all over the place warning us to "cover off and pick a target," but we had to wait for the order to fire or else we knew it would be him that would kill us, not the bloody gends!

Quinlan knew this could only last so long before an attack. Even though he was deprived of the big picture regarding information, he understood the ramifications of how an attack precipitated by a stray shot could be manipulated internationally for propaganda.

In order that higher authority be made aware of the situation, even though regular radio updates were being radioed in the Irish language back to Battalion HQ, Quinlan decided to send an officer back to carry his briefing on the situation personally.

Capt. Liam Donnelly, whose Support Platoon was to suffer most of the later bombardment, was selected. On September 9, with Lufira Bridge totally controlled by Katangan forces, Quinlan requested a vehicle be allowed return to Elisabethville for reasons of a medical emergency.

Capt. Donnelly reported to Battalion HQ the gravity of the situation for A Company at Jadotville. According to an account by retired officer Capt. Mick Farrell, "to Donnelly's consternation he was left cooling his heels for five precious hours while the battalion brass entertained UN supremo Conor Cruise O'Brien to dinner in the battalion mess."

Lt. Carey also recounts that Capt. Donnelly was delayed by the function in the mess for O'Brien and that no one would listen to his report.

However, he did convey to HQ that A Company was now surrounded by a large formation of troops and that Lufira was effectively blocked. He passed on Quinlan's recommendation to the Battalion Commander, Lt. Col. Hugh McNamee, that A Company be withdrawn from Jadotville or be reinforced with a much superior force.

As things stood, A Company was dug in and ready to defend itself against a force that outnumbered it over twenty to one. The Company was deployed in the following manner: In the villas nearest to town were deployed No. 1 Platoon, commanded by the pipe-smoking Lt. Joe Leech, and Support Platoon, commanded by Capt. Liam Donnelly. Support Platoon had a detachment of small sixty mm mortars under the direction of Sgt. Tom Kelly from Galway. On the other side of the road were No. 2 Platoon, commanded by Lt. Tom Quinlan (no relation to Comdt. Quinlan), and No. 3 Platoon, commanded by Lt. Noel Carey. The Headquarter Company, which included Comdt. Quinlan; his 2IC, Capt. Dermot Byrne; the two senior NCOs, C/S Jack Prendergast and CQMS Pat Neville; the medics, clerks, and cooks, was also situated between Nos. 2 and 3 Platoons.

A Company was well spread out at this stage, to try to deny tactical advantage to the Katangans, who were continually trying to encroach into the Irish-occupied area.

For Lt. Carey, the amount of ground the troops were trying to secure was a difficulty in its own right. "We covered an area of a quarter of a mile by half a mile, much too large for an infantry company."

A Company had the following armaments: Small arms consisted of the new FN automatic rifles. In addition, officers and certain NCOs carried the Gustaf submachine gun. Each platoon had three Bren light machine guns, which were to prove effective. The six sixty mm mortars under Sgt. Kelly were located in Support Platoon area and had a maximum range of eight hundred yards. There were two eighty-four mm antitank guns with a range of six hundred yards. There were also two Vickers machine guns, mounted on tripods and used for sustained fire. Each of these had an effective range of one thousand yards. These weapons were belt fed and cooled by a water container attached by way of a pipe. They had been used extensively by the British Army in World War II. There were two ancient armored cars attached to A Company under the command Lt. Kevin Knightly, and each car was mounted with a Vickers machine gun.

Missing were many of the standard tools of defense. A Company had no mines, barbed wire, trip flares, or heavy mortars. In fact, the flares they did have, Verey lights—cartridges fired out of a special pistol—proved next to useless when used to try an illuminate the sky during sneak attacks at night.

Aside from the above, and unthinkable today for any modern force engaged in defending an area, A Company had no recourse to artillery support or air support, the ultimate deciding factors in any successful defense of ground.

Even the helmets issued to the men at the time were useless, being made out of a type of fiberglass and used for ceremonial or patrol duty. They were actually helmet liners and designed to be worn inside the steel helmet that normally accompanied them.

Due to malfunctions there were no radio communications between the platoons and HQ Platoon. Most of this would have to be done physically by a runner, and the only connection to HQ in Elisabethville was through a C12 radio set that was notoriously fussy about when it chose to work.

At Elisabethville, Donnelly reminded HQ of the tactical situation. The point was again made that the reasons for deployment of A Company did not now exist. There was no threat to the white population; rather, they were part of the threat against the UN forces there. During this period, Quinlan also radioed to request two more platoons of men, four armored cars, and the eighty-one mm mortars that lack of transport had earlier deprived him of.

The end result was that Quinlan got none of these things.

Understandably, this is something that all the surviving members of A Company feel substantially aggrieved about to this day.

It does seem incredible that with such reports, both by radio and by Donnelly in person, other action wasn't taken. There are no specific answers as regards this. But with the benefit of hindsight, a type of explanation perhaps can be seen to emerge. Donnelly was assured that his report had been noted and higher authority informed and that everything was under control. Donnelly returned to Jadotville with a truck full of rations and an Irish platoon to escort it. The platoon was stopped at Lufira bridge and turned back. Donnelly continued on to what he now believed to be a hopeless situation. However, he was still a platoon commander, and if battle was joined it would be him his men would look to for leadership. So, back he went and fulfilled his duty.

It should now be taken into account that Operation Morthor was in the final stages of planning. Its objective, under the guidance of Conor Cruise O'Brien, was a bold one—to restore Katanga to the Congo.

It is not the remit of this book to get into the intricacies of what led to Operation Morthor or the consequences. Suffice to say that Morthor was supposed to finish what Rumpunch had started—to pluck the teeth from the Katangan state by lifting their officers and seizing the strategic objectives they held.

In his memoirs, O'Brien states his case for doing this under two approaches. Firstly, there was the fact that the Katangan state was using Psyops and propaganda to whip up public fervor provocative of open confrontation with UN forces, and it would only be a matter of time before major bloodshed occurred. Secondly, there was the fact that O'Brien believed the additional UN resolution passed earlier in the year gave him full authority to carry out Operation Morthor in order to stop impending civil war. He also states that he had the UN Secretary-General's full knowledge of and authorization for the operation.

In light of this, it is likely that the ONUC leadership in Katanga was confident that when they bared their teeth and showed the Katangans they finally meant business, they would capitulate.

The idea of either reinforcing A Company or evacuating them would have taken resources needed for Morthor. More importantly, it would have seemed to the planners at the time that once Morthor commenced, the Katangans' attention would be diverted from Jadotville to more pressing matters.

So from this perspective, all A Company had to do was sit tight and hold the line. In a few days it would be all over, as negotiations would have become the order of the day between President Tshombe and Conor Cruise O'Brien.

A nice plan, if the Katangans had decided to play along. Of course, the denuded military intelligence-gathering capability of ONUC probably contributed to decisions taken with what now looks like entirely erroneous information.

The focus of this operation was to be in the Elisabethville area. In authorizing it, O'Brien was opening a hornets' nest, for it brought into question the UN's authority to wage war on Katanga, which is, in effect, what happened.

Operation Morthor started what historians now refer to as the First Battle of Katanga, in the early hours of September 13, 1961.

10

BOMBARDMENT

Pallid, unshaved and thirsty, blind with smoke.
Things seemed all right at first. We held their line.

—SIEGFRIED SASSOON,
"COUNTER-ATTACK"

The first A Company learned of the commencement of Operation Morthor was at 0700 hours on September 13, 1961, when a radio message was relayed to A Company informing them that all installations in Elisabethville were in UN hands.

Lt. Carey was orderly officer on the morning the message came through. "I immediately called the OC [Quinlan] in his room and he told me to inform all officers and to alert the platoons. I could only find the ambulance to use as transport."

Less than half an hour later, the Katangans launched their first attack on the A Company positions as the bulk of the troops attended Mass. It does seem like military madness that A Company was not informed of Operation Morthor and the fact it could result in an attack on the Irish positions at Jadotville.

But then it should also be noted that the UN Force commander for the entire Congo operation, Gen. Sean McKeown, is on record as saying he "was only informed of what was to happen in Elisabethville at ten o'clock" on the night preceding the proposed operation. He later stated that from the time of O'Brien's arrival in Elisabethville he had been largely sidelined and ignored.

These statements were made to Col. J. T. O'Neill during an interview with the General in Athlone in 1995. However, it should also be remembered that O'Brien, in his Katangan memoir, consistently writes highly of McKeown throughout.

O'Neill notes, however, that at a peacekeeping symposium at the Irish Army's UN School in 1995, both O'Brien and McKeown were in agreement that the order to deploy A Company to Jadotville "was a decision taken at the top"—that is, from UN HQ in New York.

Confusion and faulty communication were not confined to A Company and Jadotville. They seem to have been a consistent feature of the entire ONUC operation, from UN HQ down to the peacekeepers on the ground.

As outlined in Chapter One, the initial attack was driven off and there was a brief lull. Quinlan has been criticized for not capitalizing on this battle hiatus to engage the enemy. However, he was now faced with an unenviable choice. He could either follow his martial instincts and training in closing with the enemy and destroying him by all known means, or he could hold off. As the situation report from Elisabethville indicated that Operation Morthor had gone to plan and the UN had the upper hand, negotiations could now be taking place, and any further action by Quinlan could jeopardize the bigger picture.

It is easy to criticize, but it should be remembered that the information flowing into Battalion HQ was to prove faulty. When it would eventually reach Quinlan it tended to be out of date.

For example, the initial information transmitted, which said that the key objectives in Elisabethville were in UN hands, was incorrect.

When the Jadotville garrison radioed after the initial attack, they said, "Alert on here." The reply from HQ in Elisabethville was, "Defend yourself with maximum force, Elisabethville in our hands."

But later, when Jadotville transmitted, "We are under fire," the reply from Elisabethville was, "So are we."

This was the first indication to Jadotville that Operation Morthor was not proving as successful as had been earlier indicated. Given the information at his disposal, there are some who would regard Quinlan's restraint balanced by defensive consideration to be a model of best practice in peacekeeping.

At 1130 hours, another attack began on A Company's positions. This time there would be no cavalier jeeps swarming the position. In classic military mode the ground around the platoon trenches started to erupt, as the eighty-one mm shells came crashing down around the shoulders of the Irish.

Depending on the fuse setting on the mortar bombs, some exploded after embedding themselves into the ground and others burst in the air overhead, showering the area with the type of white-hot deadly shrapnel the medics later dug out of Wally Hegarty's back.

In addition to the mortar fire there was also a French seventy-five mm field gun which was trained on the Irish positions and was now busily raining shells down upon them.

Undoubtedly, without the time spent preparing well-fortified trenches with overhead cover for shell burst, many of A Company would have been left as filling for body bags.

While the temptation for the Irish troops to bury themselves at the bottom of their trenches must have been immense since hardly any of them would have been subjected to such an intense bombardment in their lives, they manned their posts and awaited the infantry assault.

For the last couple of decades, Irish troops going abroad on active service have experienced what is called a "battle inoculation." The idea is to put the troops in trenches in a reasonably safe state and subject them to shell and machine-gun fire.

There are two reasons for this. The first is to attune their ear to the different caliber of weapons being brought to bear on them. The second is to acclimatize the soldier to the initial terror such a noisy onslaught can cause.

To their immense credit, the troops of A Company, untried and surrounded as they were, stood their ground. Again, the credit for this must go to Quinlan's continuous training regime and the standard of junior leadership.

As John Gorman put it:

When lads were being bombarded in the trenches they looked to their corporals and sergeants for guidance, and if they weren't afraid, then neither were we. Of course I was lucky. I was set work in the stores with CQMS Neville. He was as steady as a rock. He was issuing so many instructions to me I didn't have any time to be afraid.

Of course, from the NCO's perspective it was a little different. Sgt. Walter Hegarty:

I wasn't much older than the lads under me. In some cases, they were older than me. But when you have people depending on you for leadership and guidance…Well, it's a great way of taking you away from your own fear.

Something that was of definite assistance in helping the company in its defense planning and may have saved lives was the information given by Charles Kearney and friends.

Sgt. Hegarty wrote about why he and the rest of A Company

were safe in their trenches when the first shells landed. Referring to the day before the initial attack, he says, "That very afternoon a friend [Kearney] brought word that a seventy-five mm [field gun or cannon] was trained on us from the golf links three quarters of a mile away. Later still he brought large scale maps showing the exact position, bless him."

The next day Hegarty again refers to Kearney's timely information to his countrymen. "We got a phone call from our friend telling us to expect an attack at 1130 hours. His information was dead accurate; they opened up with their mortars."

At this point it should be noted that the phone lines were still open to the villas in the Purfina garage area. This was a double-edged sword for Quinlan and A Company. Up until the morning battle commenced, the garage owner, a Belgian, was still in situ.

It was later learned that this man had been reporting directly to de Clary, the mercenary OC, on the Irish preparations and the routine of morning Mass. Thus they had chosen the ideal time for their initial sneak attack.

By keeping the phone lines open, it meant that Kearney was able to update Quinlan somewhat on operational developments. However, the Katangans also used the phone line to tell Quinlan constantly how hopeless his situation was.

The Burgomaster even rang at one point to threaten that a civilian mob would attack the positions and that Quinlan would be responsible for any deaths that might occur. Obviously mistaking the earlier Irish hesitance to open fire as a sign of weakness, the Burgomaster harangued Quinlan, saying that the deaths would be on his and the UN's conscience.

But Quinlan, at this stage briefed by Kearney on the fact that many of the civilians were well armed and taking part in the battle, replied that any mob approaching his positions would be cut down by his men.

The bombardment still continued. The bulk of enemy fire was directed at No. 1 and Support Platoon. The hapless Capt. Donnelly, it seemed, was being punished even more than most for not having saved his own skin.

The troops in No. 1 Platoon, however, recall Lt. Leech, detached as ever, calmly smoking his pipe throughout the bombardment, studying the ground like an interested bird-watcher rather than a soldier awaiting the horror of attack. It was such nonchalance in the face of extreme danger by Leech that inspired so much confidence in his men.

At some time around this point, the Irish sustained their first casualty. Pte. Bill Ready, a young fitter from Mullingar, was hit by incoming fire. He had opened fire as he saw Katangan soldiers charging toward his position.

Bill's shots alerted his comrades to the enemy's approach. But they also meant he drew fire. A bullet went through his right thigh and ricocheted across his stomach. Fortunately, a spare magazine strapped to his chest stopped a second bullet finishing him off.

But the round was a tracer—a bullet which ignites so the firer can see where his shots are landing. So not only did Ready sustain a gunshot wound to his thigh and grazing to his chest, but his webbing started to go on fire. Before the unit medic, Pte. Broderick, could staunch the blood-flow from Ready's thigh, he had to douse the flames.

A field dressing was slapped on the young fitter's leg and he was propped up in a trench with his Gustaf pointed to the front as the Katangans regrouped to attack.

And attack they did. For Lt. Carey and the men of No. 3 Platoon, it was a chance to get into the fight proper:

At this time there was a shout from my forward trenches that troops were advancing across the scrub in our direction. I ran to the front trench and gave orders to open fire, even though in the excitement I could not make out the enemy.

Eventually the Katangan troops were identified and I grabbed the Bren gun and commenced firing, as we could now see the enemy at about six hundred yards distance... As I did so, the trenches of No. 2 Platoon opened up with their Bren gun and small arms...It was obvious some Katangans were hit and the others quickly dispersed towards the town.

We were elated at our success, but could still hear mortar and machine-gun fire directed at our forward platoons and we hoped they were well and holding out.

Sgt. Hegarty was later to lavish praise on the young lieutenant when he learned that "during the encounter Carey manned the LA [Light Automatic—that is, the Bren gun] *night and day*, snatched the odd hour's sleep, and gave heart to all in sight."

For many of A Company, the fight was now taking on a personal dimension. In the distance, the troops could make out armed civilians arriving to the gendarmerie lines. These were the very people they had been sent to protect.

"The people there didn't want UN protection and had more in common with the Belgian-led rebels. They detested us," recalls Sgt. Bobby Allen, (then corporal) now eighty, who returned to the Congo in 1962 for a second tour of duty, during which he was to be awarded the Distinguished Service Medal.

He recalls seeing waves of up to six hundred native Katangan soldiers charging the Irish positions. "There were mountains of them coming at us. They weren't very well trained but there were so many and they just kept coming."

Bob became a well-known figure as cook-corporal, delivering what became known as "Jadotville stew" to the men in the trenches each day. As he did this, he was often under fire. He was later to play a leading role in assisting a helicopter to land under fire.

By now many of the Irish were eager to get to close quarters with the attacking infantry. As John Gorman put it, "After being under mortar and machine-gun fire we were aching for a crack at them, to get to them up close."

Indeed, at about this time, the forward platoons were about to implement the old adage, "payback is a bitch." After being on the receiving end of the eighty-one mm mortars for most of the morning, Sgt. Tom Kelly organized a riposte of his own.

No doubt helped by Kearney's earlier information, Kelly, exposing himself to enemy fire, managed to coordinate his mortar fire onto the position of the opposing seventy-five mm.

To quote eyewitness Sgt. Hegarty, "Three rounds later they went up in a shower of debris." It is believed that Kelly's accurate mortar fire managed to hit the ammunition resupply area behind the enemy guns, thus causing maximum damage to gun and crew and gaining a breathing space for his comrades.

The Katangan onslaught began to ease off later that afternoon, around 1500 hours, after the Irish had successfully repulsed a six-hundred-strong infantry attack. With the retreat of the Katangan infantry came sporadic rifle fire on the Irish trenches.

It appeared that during the infantry attack, some snipers had managed to infiltrate some of the unoccupied villas in the Support Platoon area of the Irish lines. This intermittent sniper fire was starting to become more of a problem until Sgt. John Monaghan came on the scene.

Monaghan had already been in the thick of action since being the first one to open fire and spoil the Katangans' attempt at a surprise attack. Now he exposed himself to enemy fire again when he moved forward with his eighty-four mm antitank gun and obliterated the house where the snipers were located.

Following this action, things bizarrely settled to the point where the Katangans requested a cease-fire to collect battlefield casualties. Quinlan, in chivalrous fashion, agreed to this.

Later, however, as dusk enveloped the Jadotville hinterland, the thump of heavy weapons could be heard coming from the Lufira bridge area.

During this period there were frantic, if garbled, radio transmissions between A Company and HQ in Elisabethville.

Earlier in the day, Jadotville had sent the message, "Enemy attack has commenced, please send strong reinforcements immediately."

Elisabethville replied. "Reinforcements at bridge. Can you contact them?"

There were then several attempts by both Elisabethville and Jadotville to contact the reinforcements, but to no avail. At 1835 hours, a relief force of mainly Irish troops with Swedish armored personnel carrier support tried to break through. The force was under the command of Comdt. Johnny Kane, another Kerryman, this time from Dingle.

This combined unit was a reinforced company—it had more troops and better firepower than a normal company. Designated Force Kane One, it was faced with the task of breaking through to the beleaguered A Company and ending the siege.

But at this stage, Force Kane One encountered heavy fire at Lufira, and were having no success in their attempts to overcome it.

They radioed Elisabethville, saying, "Putting in final attack. Must return to E'ville if not successful."

Elisabethville replied, "Inflict as many casualties and do as much damage to enemy as possible."

Meanwhile, at Jadotville, the Irish could hear the action and felt sure their comrades would soon be breaking through to reach them. Lt. Carey sums up the feelings of many of A Company at this time when he recounts:

Then, to our delight, we heard the explosions of heavy mortars and firing at the Lufira bridge. It was a great feeling that after acquitting ourselves well we were going to be rescued by our colleagues from the battalion.

After about an hour, there was no noise from the bridge and we prepared to greet our rescuers. We waited and waited and waited, and as darkness drew in it became obvious that we were not to be rescued that night. Speculation that they had rested up until first light and would be with us the next day sustained us for the moment.

11

WAR OF ATTRITION

We've fought with many men across the seas,
An' some of 'em was brave an' some was not.

—RUDYARD KIPLING,
"FUZZY-WUZZY"

It would be nearly three days before Force Kane Two would try again to breakthrough to A Company. This attempt was also doomed to failure and a number of fatalities would be suffered.

It has been argued that agreeing to the cease-fire allowed more Katangan troops to be diverted to the bridge. However, the cease-fire didn't last that long. According to Quinlan's personal report:

They sent ambulances to collect their dead and wounded out of this building [the one destroyed by Sgt. Monaghan and his antitank crew] and immediately [when] that mission was accomplished they opened fire again without warning.

Small arms and machine-gun fire were to be exchanged throughout the night. However, Quinlan knew that his position, as it was, would not be tenable if a significant attacking force were to breach it:

> I decided to withdraw our forward platoon at last light into a new defensive position. We got every man who could be spared to dig trenches in the new position. At last light we thinned out the forward positions and one hour after last light our new position was fully organized.

By carrying out this shrewd maneuver, Quinlan had consolidated his forces and ensured their survival for another few days. By keeping them spread out originally he had managed to inflict significant damage on the enemy before they were able to close with the Irish troops.

Judicious use of the few support weapons available to him had meant Quinlan had been able to break up the enemy attacks before they got close enough to secret themselves in the thick bush surrounding the Irish position.

The armored cars, Vickers machine guns and sixty mm mortars had enabled Quinlan to conduct an offensive form of defense that had penetrated the enemy's lines.

His support weapons had destroyed at least three enemy mortar crews that day, and only one of his men had been wounded.

However, Quinlan knew this couldn't last. With the greater resources and weight of numbers, they would have eventually got through his lines. Once penetrated, the Irish lines would have been impossible to defend.

A Company was already strung out across an area much bigger than what a company would normally be expected to defend. The new defensive position was now 250 yards by 120 yards on reasonably high ground. It enabled A Company to detect enemy movement on rising ground from 600 to 1,500 yards.

Unfortunately, the weakest point in the company's defense was the area they had originally been expected to defend—Jadotville town. To the company's rear on the Elisabethville road the Irish troops had little or no opportunity for observation, and a hill about three hundred feet high, approximately one mile to their rear, was held by the gendarmerie. This hill gave the Katangans a distinct advantage, affording them high ground from which to observe and fire upon the Irish positions.

Even so, morale was high. The men had great confidence in Quinlan's leadership and trusted him implicitly. As far as Sgt. Walter Hegarty was concerned, by the end of the first day's fighting, "Comdt. Quinlan grew to giant size in every man's eyes."

During the brief cease-fire, Lt. Carey had taken the opportunity to meet up with his fellow platoon commanders. Quinlan called a rapid conference to appraise his officers and senior NCOs of the tactical situation.

The exuberance of the younger officers seemed hard to abate. They had survived their first taste of real action, driven back a superior enemy, and were now awaiting a relief force that had broken through Lufira bridge … or so they thought.

Quinlan soon doused these fires of exuberance when he told them the news. Battalion HQ had just informed him, he told the speechless group, that the relief column had been recalled to Elisabethville.

For Noel Carey it was like a kick in the solar plexus. "We were shocked. They could not do this to their fellow soldiers. There must be a mistake. Maybe it's a ploy and they will attack again at first light."

As the stunned young officer digested the news, the cooks arrived with what was to be the soldiers' first meal for the entire day. Carey noted Quinlan's demeanor following the delivery of his bad news. "[He] was obviously disgusted but told us to ensure that morale was maintained and, after a meal of stew provided by our heroic cooks...I returned to my trench."

To this day, many members of A Company harbor grudges against Force Kane for not breaking through. But, as we shall later see, the situation was anything but a simple issue of black and white.

0525 hours on Thursday, September 14, and the men of A Company awoke to a breakfast of eighty-one mm mortar rounds crashing in around their trenches.

The mortar fire was recorded as being "very heavy and very accurate." It was accompanied by heavy machine-gun fire, and it was to be nearly an hour before the Irish troops found out where the fire was coming from.

Finally, a position was pinpointed at a grove nine-hundred yards from the Irish positions. Again Sgt. Tom Kelly proved his skill as a mortar man when his little detachment of sixty mm mortars replied.

Kelly's counter-bombardment destroyed the enemy mortars and the crews were "cut down by armored cars and light automatics as they tried to run away." There was no doubt that both sides were engaged in a bitter fight.

In the earlier stages of the conflict, however, sources in A Company record that the attached chaplain, Fr. Thomas Fagan, had attempted to persuade troops and officers not to open fire as the Irish were "here on a mission of peace."

However misguided the Chaplain was in attempting to interfere with soldiers being instructed in the defense of their positions, he was probably just exhibiting the typical Irish citizen's ignorance of these matters, assuming peacekeeping missions meant an atmosphere of continuous sweetness and light. In any event, Fr. Fagan did not neglect his duty to the men.

Following the success of Sgt. Kelly's sixty mm mortars and

Lt. Knightly's armored cars, the Katangans developed new tactics. They would lob a few mortar rounds at the Irish and quickly move position. While A Company was still under fire, this tactic lessened the Katangans' accuracy considerably.

But then, at 1300 hours, just in time for a dose of Jadotville stew, a new player entered the fray in the person of Jacques Delen, a French mercenary fighter pilot.

Delen was a part of the fledgling Katangan air force which was commanded by a South African mercenary named Jeremiah Puren. Puren wasn't a pilot, and the force he commanded wasn't exactly the Luftwaffe.

This "air force" consisted of a German Dornier bomber of WWI vintage, a helicopter out of which the pilot tossed hand grenades and, most importantly of all, two Fouga Magister jet fighters.

In some accounts of the Congo operation these jets are described as "aged," but, considering the Irish Air Corps were still using them operationally into the 1990s, the ones in the Congo were in pretty good order.

In any event, the UN had no airpower available to counter this threat at that time. By late September, Indian bombers and Swedish and Ethiopian fighters arrived in-country to give the UN air primacy.

But that was to be all too late for A Company. The gendarmerie at Jadotville may only have had recourse to one aircraft, but "In the land of the blind, the one-eyed man is king."

The Fouga swooped in over the Irish trenches, and A Company got the shock of their lives as they chomped down on their stew, which by now had degenerated to hard tack biscuits and hot vegetable water. The first overflight was just reconnaissance, and the pilot merrily waved at the troops below. But when he returned it was a different story. None of the Irish had ever experienced an air attack before, and, as Sgt. Walter Hegarty says, they had no idea what to expect:

It came back at 1545 hours and dropped two bombs and gave us two runs [that is, the pilot strafed the positions with his automatic cannon]. That guy terrorized me. He came back at 1745 with two more bombs but chanced only one strafing run in the teeth of company fire.

By the last strafing run, the troops were better prepared. Quinlan, while being equipped with no antiaircraft guns, coordinated all small-arms, machine-gun, and armored-car fire on the jet. This is what Hegarty means when he mentions "company fire."

Despite some claims to the contrary, A Company did not manage to take down the jet, but they did make the pilot think twice about cockily flying low on bombing runs. As a result, the pilot's accuracy suffered and lives were undoubtedly saved.

However, the bombing sorties destroyed what was left of A Company's transport, killing off any notion of a breakout to link up with Force Kane when next it came to Lufira bridge. Another bombing run resulted in a near miss for two Irish soldiers manning mortars in the weapons pit of Support Platoon. One of the bombs landed so close to the pit it caved it in, burying Pte. James Tahany, a nineteen-year-old Sligo man, alive. Twenty-one-year-old Pte. Edward Gormley, another Sligo man, was blown clear of the pit.

Only the quick thinking of Sgt. John Monaghan saved Tahany's life. Despite still being under attack, Monaghan clawed at the soil until he managed to drag a severely shocked Tahany to safety.

Monaghan, like the responsible sergeant he was, kept Tahany under his wing for the rest of the action and ensured his trauma didn't interfere with his ability to continue fighting.

However, under continuous attack, with supplies of food and water dwindling, Irish morale began to sap. It fell to men like Monaghan to lighten the atmosphere.

During a brief lull in the fighting, Monaghan turned to his

platoon commander, Lt. Joe Leech, asking him to "Sign this, please, sir."

Leech opened the sheet to discover it was an official request for a weekend pass. Struck by the sheer defiance of adversity being demonstrated by Monaghan, Lt. Leech playfully leapt out of his trench to chase the sergeant in a mock show of rage.

This impromptu sketch was accompanied by the cheers and shouts of their fellow soldiers in other trenches. But within minutes it was back to business, as the Katangans launched another attack.

Civilian technician Charles Kearney was still sending information through to Quinlan. In a written report following the siege at Jadotville, Kearney estimated the Katangan forces at between four thousand and five thousand. In the early hours of the attack, the Irish had repulsed waves of gendarmes up to six hundred strong.

While A Company was experiencing such drama, their loved ones back in Ireland were undergoing their own ordeal.

BBC World Service reports at the time estimated falsely that at least fifty to sixty Irish had been killed in the fighting. Indeed, both national and international newspapers were full of stories about the Irish casualties suffered.

Many years later, veterans told me they believed this error had occurred because the pilot of the jet had mistaken bedding rolls behind trenches for body bags.

But given the manipulative circumstances that caused A Company to be deployed to Jadotville, it is much more likely the Katangan Ministry of Information was busy disseminating heartbreak stories in order to manipulate world opinion to its own ends.

To some extent, it very nearly had the desired effect. As the stories reached Ireland of the besieged garrison, heretical as it may seem now, talk began quietly in government circles of pulling out the troops.

This is recorded, as a matter of fact, in the *Peacekeeper's Handbook*:

The effect in Ireland was immediate and the Irish Government was forced to consider withdrawing from ONUC. On investigation it was found that the reports of heavy casualties were quite untrue, but the damage had been done and for a period the political support for the UN operation was in some jeopardy.

This statement alone demonstrates how the Jadotville action had morphed from a tactical problem for part of ONUC into a strategic one for both the UN and the Irish government.

The Government took the issue so seriously that Taoiseach Seán Lemass dispatched Minister for External Affairs Frank Aiken to the Congo to find out what exactly was going on. It seems incredible to think the Irish government was excluded from the information loop on the Jadotville situation, especially when there had been no reports of fatalities radioed back from Jadotville to Battalion HQ.

Journalist Cathal O'Shannon, then an *Irish Times* reporter who had been covering the Irish in the Congo, remembers Aiken talking to senior officers before they left for Africa:

He was talking to a group of senior officers and told them they should do anything to save the lives of the troops. Aiken was scared that Irish soldiers would be killed. He seemed to want to imbue these officers with a sense of caution, to do anything except raise their rifles.

It would have been an almighty coup on the world stage if the Katangans had forced the Irish contingent to slink off the international stage with their tail between their legs. They were already doing a magnificent job of portraying the UN as the aggressor, and to get a Western nation to pull out of ONUC would have sealed the fate of the operation.

The Irish government were already concerned that their troops were being drawn into a situation where an external political solution was being forced upon Katanga. This was something they had wanted to avoid, believing that any political solutions must come from the Congolese themselves.

But all these considerations were academic to the troops of A Company. Now marooned, running low on ammunition and on half rations, they clung on glumly to their positions, resolved to look whatever fate had in store for them squarely in the eye.

Sgt. Hegarty had become one of the next Irish casualties following his altercation with the two mortar bombs. Although he made it into a trench he was rapidly going into shock. Ever the professional, he realized what was happening, wrapped himself in blankets and sought out the medic:

> After primary shock and during a lull in the firing, with Brod-erick's help I staggered off towards Company HQ lines with ambitions to reach the Medical Officer [Comdt. Joe Clune]. After one hundred yards I was down with weakness [at this point Hegarty's back, buttocks, and legs had been opened with shrapnel, and he would have lost a fair amount of blood] and had to be stretched, fully conscious but very embarrassed.

Hegarty was brought back to the Company HQ, where he was shot full of morphine and put into a delirium of sorts. CQMS Pat Neville, who was looking out for everyone's physical welfare, recalls Hegarty being brought in to the improvised aid station he had set up:

> He was doped up on morphine, but he was bawling out for his weapon and demanding it be returned to him. Actually he was lying on it at the time. We thought it best not to bother him about that.

After treatment he refused to stay in sick bay and returned to his platoon and the fighting.

CQMS Neville goes on to describe Hegarty as "an outstanding NCO," so it was small wonder he later went on to be decorated with the DSM for action in the aftermath of Jadotville.

At this point Quinlan was waging his own personal war. Aside from the mortar rounds, shells, and machine-gun fire raging around him, the Company Commander also had the psychological pressure of regular phone calls from the local Burgomaster calling on him to surrender.

Quinlan tried to prevail on the Burgomaster's common sense and asked him to use his influence to "stop the fighting." The Burgomaster asked that he keep the phone line open.

"I agreed to this," says Quinlan in his after-action report, "foolishly perhaps, because this telephone was used as a means of waging psychological warfare. Each night they rang with appeals and threats of all sorts and asking for our immediate surrender…I informed him that surrender was out of the question."

Quinlan even had calls from a man purporting to be a member of the Red Cross and trying to convince the Irish to give up in the interest of saving lives.

However, later that day, two gendarmes ended up owing their lives to the Irish. A perimeter patrol checking for infiltrators during an ease in the fighting that evening apprehended two mercenaries.

The two men were Pierre van der Wegen and Michael Paucheun, both dressed in civilian clothes and carrying two machine guns, two FN rifles, grenades, and revolvers. Paucheun was a mercenary officer and is believed to have been Belgian. Van der Wegen was an ex-Foreign Legion para and, though in civvies, still carried his Legion beret.

When both men were apprehended, CQMS Neville was on

the scene. As the quartermaster sergeant, he was responsible for safeguarding prisoners. They claimed they had come from Elisabeth-ville, where they had been told by President Tshombe that an Irish company had been taken prisoner at Jadotville and were to be used as hostages by the Katangan government in negotiations with the UN.

This further underlines how the isolation of A Company at Jadotville was now completely undermining the entire ONUC mission in Katanga. However, the two mercenaries were fortunate to become prisoners. As CQMS Neville remembers it:

> When we caught them, they were armed and in civilian clothes, highly irregular in a theater of war, but this was somewhere between war and peace. The rules weren't quite the same.

> Anyway, the officer on the spot (I'd prefer not to name the man) was enraged at the two mercenaries. He'd been dead on his feet assisting in the defense of the area and we were all feeling a bit let down when no relief force arrived.

> So when we lifted the two boys, the officer ordered them to stand apart from everybody and announced he was going to shoot them as spies. Everyone was shocked except, it seemed, the two mercenaries, who appeared to accept it as part of the fortunes of war.

> As the officer made ready to carry out his intention I stood in front of the two mercenaries. I said to him "Sir, for God's sake, you're doing a marvelous job. Don't go and do something you'll regret for the rest of your life. Look, I'm the CQMS, I'm responsible for these lads' welfare, and I'm taking them in as prisoners."

At that point he saw sense. He was a good man and a great officer and that's why I'll never name him. He doesn't deserve that. The frustrations of battle affect us all in different ways.

The two mercenaries were taken into custody and Neville told them he was going to be responsible for them. "Thank you, Sergeant Major," said Paucheun, "but I have one request. My comrade is upset. His beret has been taken from him and these things are very dear to ex-Legion paras."

So CQMS Neville had the beret returned, though he was mildly surprised that the prospect of losing it had upset the mercenary more than the prospect of losing his life.

"When it was all over and we were back in Elisabethville, I met Paucheun on the street. He was in full uniform and appeared to be a very senior rank. He handed me a bottle of champagne and said, 'For you, Sergeant Major. Thank you for looking after us.'"

Through Thursday and Friday the enemy made up to ten attacks on A Company's positions. On Thursday night the Irish suffered their fifth casualty, Pte. John Manning, the soldier whose letters home grace the pages of this book.

That night, the gendarmerie had managed to get within twenty yards of the Irish positions. John Gorman was manning a Bren gun with his comrade Michael "Butch" Brennan.

The two young soldiers were dug in on an anthill covering the enemy approaches into the camp. They stayed at this station until hostilities ceased, assisting in cutting down assaulting enemy troops.

John Gorman remembers Manning getting hit:

There had been a flurry of shooting from up really close and we thought we had seen them off. But then a sniper took a shot at Manning. It was from close by in one of the villas.

C/S Prendergast was on the scene immediately. While the lads put a dressing on Manning's shoulder, Prenders just asked, "Where?" and Manning indicated the villa the shot came from. Quick as a flash, Prenders was over to it and lobbing in grenades. He finished off the rest with machine-gun fire. We had no more trouble that night.

The Katangans again requested a cease-fire from Quinlan that night, which he refused. The company officers then held a meeting, where Quinlan informed them that Battalion HQ had "urged us to hold on".

As far as Lt. Noel Carey was concerned, "the troops were sound and were prepared for a longer fight, and morale was very high. This was echoed by all the platoon commanders, but we did have interference from the Chaplain. He stressed we were on a peaceful mission and not at war. 'Tell that to the Katangans,' I thought."

Friday morning came with what was now the usual cacophony of machine guns and mortars. Another attack was repulsed by both small arms and sixty mm mortar fire. However, No. 3 Platoon, commanded by Lt. Carey, was now being successfully bracketed by mortar fire.

Carey ordered his men back to the rear trenches for their safety. He, however, stayed on to man the Bren gun and be the first point of defense if the enemy tried a sneak infantry assault on the heels of the barrage.

As they withdrew I was left on my own in a deserted trench with mortar fire falling all round me. It was a frightening experience as I expected to be the next victim of mortar fire.

I even put a sandbag on my head to prevent shrapnel penetrating my helmet. As I sat there in the trench, all alone, I thought of my family at home and mostly about Angela and how I would miss her if I was killed. It was one of the worst moments of the battle.

Despite the terror and fatigue, Lt. Carey was to have his mood lifted by his radio man, Pte. Myler. In the midst of lead flying around during one of the attacks, Myler asked Carey, "Sir, do you think it would be anything like this in a real war?"

Before an incredulous Carey could answer, Myler, oblivious to the chaos around him, answered his own question, "No, if this was a real war, we'd be wearing grenades in our belts."

Another anomaly of the whole Jadotville saga was the little old Belgian lady who lived in a house just across from the villa A Company were using for an HQ. Why she had not vacated her house nobody knows. Quinlan had offered to arrange a safe departure for her but she refused. However, throughout the fighting she made cakes and potato crisps for the troops. She also constantly urged the Irish not to be downcast at the taunts and threats that were leveled at them.

By Saturday, food and water were nearly out and ammunition was running dangerously low. Fatigue and lack of sleep were now major factors for the troops trying to keep focused and alert.

The Irish could see bodies being carried off the battlefield by their enemies. So far they had been lucky with their own casualties. But how long could that luck hold?

Now another enemy began to hack at the Irish defense—thirst. One attempt was made to resupply the besieged Irish with water. A gutsy Norwegian helicopter pilot named Lt. Bjarne Hovden volunteered to fly a supply of water to the parched troops. Hovden was taking an extreme risk because the Katangans were being supported by the Fouga jet, flown by Delen, a former fighter pilot.

Fortunately, the jet was busy attacking Elisabethville and later

Force Kane Two. Accompanying Hovden as copilot was Warrant Officer Eric Thors, from Sweden. The helicopter had developed engine trouble and was having difficulty finding a place to land.

Realizing his predicament, CQMS Pat Neville and Cpl. Bob Allen dashed out of cover to lay sheets down as markers on even ground for Hovden to land safely.

There was no firing until just as the chopper landed. Then all hell broke loose. For CQMS Neville it seemed like his time had come:

> Rifles, light automatics, mortars, and heavy machine-gun fire. Everything was being fired at us. I expected to die every second. This was hell to Bobby and me…We were astonished we didn't get wounded.

By exposing themselves so recklessly to enemy fire the two NCOs had done their comrades a favor, as many of the positions of the enemy machine guns and mortars were noted, and counter-fire returned accordingly.

However, despite Hovden, Thors, Neville, and Allen all risking their lives, the whole exercise turned out to be a waste. Like a scene reminiscent of Arnhem in WWII, when a British para got killed trying to open a supply container only to find it filled with berets, the much-needed water supplies on the chopper were useless. Somebody back at HQ had used jerricans that had previously held petrol, and they hadn't been washed out properly.

Quinlan was livid. Not only were his men having to suffer further deprivation, Hovden and his copilot had risked their lives for nothing, and now they were all stuck in Jadotville until the bitter end.

The chopper was no longer airworthy. But the Katangans were severely punished by the Irish for revealing the positions of most of their recently placed support weapons.

Responding to the attack on the chopper landing site, A

Company laid down such a withering hail of accurate fire that many of the native troops fled into the jungle. A battle went on for a full two hours. After a lull occurred, with the Katangans licking their wounds, A Company bade their time and then hit them again with another full hour of sustained small-arms and support-weapon fire.

The back of the Katangan attack was well and truly broken, as was their resolve. At this point Quinlan noted that the white officers were shooting their own men in an attempt to stem the rout that was occurring in the Katangan lines.

For any other force with the option of proper resupply like the Americans in Vietnam, or the ability to project force like the British in Northern Ireland, the situation would be looking like a victory. A Company had effectively won the fire fight.

Force Kane Two, this time with the addition of an Indian Gurkha unit, made another stab at Lufira bridge. This time they received a mauling at the hands of the Katangans, and were ambushed on their return to Elisabethville.

At this point, things were becoming critical. Quinlan's meager supply of support weapons was running very short on ammunition, and it would soon be a case of bayonets and hand-to-hand combat. Coupled with this was the shortage of food.

However, morale had been efficiently maintained by CQMS Pat Neville and his cooks, who were personally risking their lives to keep the trenches supplied with what little hot food there was.

Another radio exchange with Elisabethville demonstrates how desperate the situation was:

Jadotville: Position desperate. Send reinforcements immediately.

Elisabethville: Can you break out? Can you break out on foot? We will meet you at the bridge.

Jadotville: Bridge about twenty miles away. We do not know
force between here and bridge. Unable to take all ammo and
supplies. This would be suicide. Only hope to remain here.
You reach us.

It should be remembered that Quinlan's transport was all now
completely destroyed. He was outnumbered thirty to one with no
intelligence about the situation behind Katangan lines, and his men
were exhausted and parched.

At this point, Quinlan must have known that the fate of A
Company was in his hands alone. There was no aid to come, no
magic options to save the day.

His orders were completely irrelevant now and it must have seemed
to him that he and his men were irrelevant to higher authority. But
he had the upper hand at the moment. The Katangans were seeking a
cease-fire, and he could accede to it from a position of strength.

But that strength was only conditional on reinforcements,
resupply, and air support. Quinlan was promised all of these at some
stage or other during the Jadotville engagement, but none of it mate-
rialized, no matter how much he advised HQ of the situation.

Should he now order his men to fight to the last in the name
of some vague concept of international law which, it now seemed,
might not even have legal validity? How would he tell grieving
mothers, widows, and girlfriends that their men had been slaughtered because the people at the very top were being outfoxed by more
focused adversaries?

If Quinlan had a specific objective or definite orders he might
have acted differently, but he was cut off from any proper direction
or advice. He could only guess from the garbled radio messages at
what the general situation was throughout the rest of Katanga.

Once he received the message that Force Kane Two had returned
to Elisabethville for a second and final time, Quinlan knew the game

was up. It was up to him now to ensure that the senseless slaughter of his men did not take place. He was their CO after all, their leader. In fact, he was all they had.

With all of this on his mind, Quinlan was approached by the Burgomaster to consider another cease-fire.

When this was passed on to Elisabethville, A Company was told that a general cease-fire was being negotiated in Elisabethville, and to hang on.

"This was disastrous news for us and left us in no negotiating position, as the Katangans were well aware of our plight," recalls Lt. Carey. Certainly Carey's point is correct.

With cease-fire negotiations going on in Elisabethville, there would be no further troop movements. The Katangans could regroup. Because of the faulty communication and intelligence system, Quinlan had no knowledge of just how tense things had become between the white officers and the native troops.

If the UN had been more active in trying to manage native perception by radio broadcasts, things would certainly have been different. If the intelligence-gathering system was in place, then perhaps broadcasts could have helped stoke the native unrest in the gendarmerie and had them cooperate with UN forces.

Even if basic tactical intelligence had been disseminated to A Company, perhaps Quinlan would have been able to see the cards he was dealt properly. But the "clean hands" policy so beloved of Dag Hammarskjöld ensured that A Company would be the ones to have to get their hands dirty.

A cease-fire was agreed between A Company and the Katangans, with both parties jointly patrolling the Jadotville area. But of course, the Katangans started to violate aspects of the agreement as soon as their strength started to grow again.

Although they didn't know it at the time, this was to be the end of the line for A Company.

12

FORCE KANE AT LUFIRA

We're foot-slog-slog-slog-sloggin' over Africa—
Foot-foot-foot-foot-sloggin' over Africa—
(Boots-boots-boots-boots-movin' up and down again!)
There's no discharge in the war!

—RUDYARD KIPLING,
"BOOTS"

According to John Gorman, Comdt. Quinlan had to be pulled off Comdt. Kane when A Company was released in a prisoner exchange in late October. "I remember when we got off the transport back in Elisabethville, Quinlan saw Johnny Kane and he went for him. A Westmeath soldier named Simon Finlass had to pull Quinlan off Kane."

A number of critical issues arise at this juncture that still cause the blood pressure to rise amongst some of the veterans who were either at Jadotville or Lufira. Chief among these is the question of who bears the bigger brunt of fault for the fall of Jadotville.

Most of the men in A Company felt let down at the time by Force Kane. But the truth of the matter is the men of Force Kane were out on a limb as much as A Company.

Comdt. Johnny Kane, an artillery corps officer back in Ireland, was given the task of leading the attempt to break through to Jadotville on September 13. Force Kane One, as the scratch unit was designated, was a hastily assembled group of troops from platoons in B Company, the Support Platoon at Battalion HQ, and armored-car detachment.

Upon assembly, they raced in a hotchpotch of vehicles to try to cross Lufira and get through to their comrades in Jadotville.

They were accompanied by medics and APCs from the Swedish contingent. Many of the Irish troops were traveling in soft-skinned buses with the windows knocked out lest they come under fire.

By the time Kane got his orders and assembled his troops it was getting near dusk. By the time he reached the bridge it was dark. The bridge was blocked with machinery, including a tractor and bulldozer, and tree trunks.

Capt. Mark Carroll tried first to get his armored car to negotiate the obstacles on the bridge. A Swedish armored car tried to assist, but both got stuck on the bridge between obstacles. They then came under withering fire from the Katangan side of the river.

Only prompt action from Capt. Carroll, who dismounted to free the vehicles from their obstacles, saved both crews as an onslaught of fire was brought to bear on the bridge by the gendarmerie when they realized the vehicles were stuck.

Despairing of any more attempts to cross at night, Force Kane withdrew a safe distance and at first light tried again. But this time the Katangans had consolidated their position and brought severe fire down on the hapless UN troops.

There has been much criticism of Kane for not pushing on through the barricades, for pulling back too far and letting the

Katangans increase their forces on the other side of the river. But most of this is unjustified.

Kane may have made some genuine errors when he made his initial estimate of the situation. But anyone who has ever served or studied warfare knows that when the first rounds fly, the operation may take many turns one never anticipates.

In fairness to Kane, it was a brave attempt to cross an obstacle-laden bridge in total darkness in the first place. Had the bridge been booby-trapped, he could have lost a substantial portion of his force; and had the Katangans brought an antitank gun to bear, he could have suffered debilitating damage.

However, Kane was dogged by the same problem as most other UN soldiers in the Congo—a total disregard by the UN leadership in the utility and coordination of intelligence gathering.

There was also the fundamental inability of Hammarskjöld, Bunche, and O'Brien to understand that for an army to function as one it must be equipped as one, not as a paramilitary police force. Changing the mandate is not enough if you don't have the necessary military hardware to project force.

Force Kane Two returned to Lufira for a last ditch attempt on Saturday, the morning of September 16. This time, despite the addition of battle-hardened Gurkha troops, they had to contend with the Fouga diving down on unopposed strafing runs, and a much larger Katangan force.

A Swedish officer described the second attempt to break through, saying, "From the military viewpoint the venture is dangerous, but from the heart it is very necessary."

Things were going to be hard enough for Force Kane Two, but the task became next to impossible when the crazy mercenary pilot, Jacques Delen, joined the action.

Delen was so confident of being unopposed in his attacks that during bombing runs on Elisabethville he would ask the airport control tower, "How am I doing? That was a good one! See you in the afternoon for more fun."

It would also seem remarkable that the leadership of ONUC did not elect to wait for their own air assets when the Katangans actually outgunned them on that score.

Conor Cruise O'Brien probably summed up the problem of the top-level UN decision-makers when he stated, "I'm a total civilian," when it came to making decisions regarding military-related matters.

Force Kane Two consisted of three hundred Irish and Indian Gurkha troops with Irish and Swedish armored car support. The column came under attack by the Fouga almost immediately, the first casualty being fifty-one-year-old Sgt. Joe Gallagher.

He was evacuated back to Elisabethville and the column wound its way along. At this point there were no other bridges to cross over— the Katangans had blown them all. In short, the UN leadership, by their ponderous decision-making, had handed the initiative in the battle directly to the Katangans.

So, of course, the Katangans had directed all their firepower at the only place Force Kane Two could cross. An attempt by Gurkha infantry, accompanied by Irish armored cars, to make a lightning dash across the bridge, ramming all obstacles, was stopped in its tracks by attack from the jet.

Three of the Indians were killed outright and eight other soldiers were wounded. Having taken a pounding, both from the jet and the heavy Katangan fire on the other side of the bridge, Force Kane withdrew in good order to Elisabethville.

However, the Katangans were not worried about letting their operational planning be intelligence-led. After all they couldn't have dirty hands when it was they that were dominating the media world, presenting themselves as plucky David to the ONUC's Goliath.

Thus, even though Force Kane had finished with Lufira, the Katangans had not finished with Force Kane. As the weary and battle-rattled UN troops returned to Elisabethville, the mercenary-led Katangans sprung a trap from either side of the road.

The first the combined UN force knew of this was when a mine exploded in front of one of the leading buses (Force Kane still had to resort to soft-skinned civilian transport for most of the troops).

The column was caught like a rabbit in the headlights of an oncoming juggernaut. Up to five Irish soldiers were wounded in the blanket of bullets that enveloped them. One man had his weapon shot out of his hands. The Irish troops sustained gunshot wounds in the stomach, back, legs, and torso. It seems miraculous that not one of them lost his life.

Another was making to return fire from a mounted machine gun when he was spun right around from the impact of a round going clean through his right leg and up his right arm. As he went down, he was still trying to fire his machine gun at the marauding Katangans.

The Indians were also to incur four casualties and one fatality.

As if Force Kane hadn't been battered enough, just as the vehicles were approaching Elisabethville, two of them collided, causing two more Indians and eight others to be injured.

Following the troops' return to Elisabethville, there was some consideration given to trying a night flanking attack. However, this was not deemed possible, as the combat engineers estimated that it would take nearly three hours to repair damage to just one of the roads needed.

Any claim that Force Kane One and Two didn't make the effort and that they didn't suffer in making it is quite clearly untrue.

Even if they had made it across the bridge there is still no guarantee they would have linked up successfully on Saturday with A Company. Granted, Force Kane Two was made up of two infantry companies and two armored sections, over three hundred men, but the bridge area had been well reinforced by then and the Fouga had a free run.

Had it been Force Kane Two that had been deployed the first time, before the Katangans had been prepared, there may have been some chance.

Granted, there may have been tactical errors made in the heat of battle. There are some who are critical of Comdt. Kane for not trying harder on the first attempt, or for pulling back too far on the first night and giving the initiative to the Katangans.

But it should be remembered that the upper echelons of the UN leadership were also blundering by not properly utilizing all the assets at their disposal. In particular, they were making no real or coordinated attempt to mobilize public opinion.

There were some attempts at radio broadcasts by Conor Cruise O'Brien's deputy, Michel Tombelaine. But there were issues with ONUC HQ in Léopoldville about the content of the broadcasts and what did or didn't constitute propaganda.

We have already discussed the dearth of intelligence-gathering activity. Granted, earlier in the year a Military Information Bureau (MIB) had been established at ONUC HQ, but it didn't have many resources. Given that O'Brien, as UN Special Representative in charge in Katanga, doesn't even mention it in his Katangan memoir, one can only conclude that it didn't make much of an impression in Katanga.

The bottom line was that mistakes were made because the leadership coming from the top was so ineffectual, particularly in utilizing standard military procedures in an operational theater. In fact, even what constituted "an operational theater" was in dispute.

The idea of civilian primacy is a bedrock of UN philosophy, and over the years some lessons have been learned. But in the Congo, it was a case of too much philosophical aspiration and not enough application of the correct tools to do the job.

But then, at times, even the job was open to debate. Was the objective of the whole business to prevent civil war at all costs and stop another front of the Cold War opening up? Or was it, more simply, to prevent civilian massacres and provide a stable environment for a political solution to be found internally? To this day, no one is too sure.

One thing we can be sure of, though, is that to troops on the ground who need clear information to attain defined objectives, this must have seemed like well-meant dithering. Neither clear information nor a defined objective was available to the men at Lufira or Jadotville.

Both units were poorly resourced in the jobs they were assigned. Both were victims of a UN leadership that was noble in its aspirations, but negligent in its duty of care to the men who served under their flag of blue.

13

CEASE-FIRE AND CAPTIVITY

My friend, you would not tell with such high zest,
To children ardent for some desperate glory,
The old Lie: Dulce et Decorum est
Pro Patria mori
[It is sweet and fitting to die for one's country].

—WILFRED OWEN,
"DULCE ET DECORUM EST"

Sunday, September 17, was a pleasant day for the troops of A Company. The sun shone and weapons were silent.

The enlisted men were in magnificent form, for hadn't they broken the back of the Katangan attack? Weren't they victorious? The Katangans had actually asked *them* for the cease-fire.

For A Company, a parallel universe was coming into being. Even though they had won the battle, they had lost the engagement. They just hadn't realized it yet.

The Katangans' initial call for a cease-fire on Saturday afternoon was to allow an ambulance to come forward and pick up the wounded from the last battle. However, Quinlan had been tipped off by Irish civilian Charles Kearney that the Katangans had been using ambulances to get up close to positions. They would then open fire on opposing forces using machine guns mounted in the back.

The Katangans again seemed anxious to demonstrate good faith and offered to pull their soldiers back from the Irish positions. Quinlan informed them that any move in any direction would result in shooting.

He then advised the Katangans that any movement should be done in an upright position and while carrying a white flag. He agreed to meet the Burgomaster and Major Michel de Clary, the gendarmerie OC, to discuss formal cease-fire terms.

However, when Katangan forces started moving without observing the agreed protocol, A Company opened fire, and a gendarmerie officer had his leg virtually severed by machine gun fire. This nearly scuppered the opportunity for a cease-fire.

The gendarmerie asked that their officers be allowed to go forward to stop the other gendarmes from continuing to fire. Quinlan refused a local cease-fire arrangement unless the jet was grounded.

He also stipulated that he would fire on any troops moving around the gendarmerie positions at Lufira bridge. Neither side seemed aware at this point that Force Kane Two had gone, never to return.

Quinlan still displayed a reasonably confident demeanor. HQ were still advising him that a relief column was in the vicinity. Gen. McKeown, the ONUC Force Commander, transmitted the following message direct to Quinlan on the Saturday:

We all here admire and commend you and your men on your gallant stand. The whole UN force and our own people and in fact the whole world are watching the outcome of your brave efforts. You have already earned yourselves the name of heroes.

Then Quinlan advised Elisabethville that Lufira bridge was mined, and that they were to await the outcome of his cease-fire talks.

Battalion HQ informed Quinlan that there were "high-level negotiations going on between the UN and the Katangans in Elisabethville." Quinlan's intention was to negotiate a local cease-fire, pending the outcome of the talks. From a strategic point of view, this was to be his downfall, as once he had ceased hostilities, he had the weaker hand.

The Katangans knew they had Quinlan between a rock and a hard place. He had agreed to the following points in the cease-fire:

1. Joint Irish-Katangan patrols would be mounted in the region, so neither side could claim a tactical advantage.

2. The Katangan forces were to return to barracks.

3. The Irish positions were to be cordoned off by a combined A Company and Katangan police detail, in order to keep sightseers from approaching the Irish positions.

4. The local police chief and Comdt. Quinlan would tour the area to reassure locals that the fighting was over.

At first A Company were riding high, convinced that a relief column was to arrive at any moment. Hopes that the cease-fire would end on UN terms were bolstered with news that three new UN fighter jets were coming and would be flying over Jadotville in a matter of days.

This, however, was a pipe dream. Apparently, Uganda wouldn't allow UN jets to traverse its airspace. Again, one has to ask what the UN thought it was doing, going onto a war footing without preparing the necessary forces.

Early on Sunday, the mercenary jet made a return to Jadotville and began buzzing the Irish trenches. Quinlan protested this, claiming, correctly, that it was a breach of the verbally agreed cease-fire.

Again, the company was led to believe through radio messages from Elisabethville that air support of some kind was on its way.

Even though the cease-fire had been just agreed, by Sunday it was plain to see the Katangans were chipping away at it bit by bit in the hope that Quinlan would not want to take up arms over frivolous little details.

The white mercenaries were still grouped around in close proximity to A Company lines and moving visibly closer. The water supply was supposed to have been restored after a French mercenary named Capt. Lasimone had turned it off during the battle. Still it had not happened. The jet was still very much in evidence in the skies.

Then a Katangan officer named Major Makita approached Quinlan and informed him that as part of the reaccommodation of Irish personnel, they would have to leave their support weapons in one villa.

At this point it is necessary to draw a picture of the general situation of how Jadotville was being perceived outside. It was far from straightforward. In his memoir *To Katanga and Back*, O'Brien makes mention of hearing that the water supply was cut off to A Company and that food was "getting scarce." He was aware on September 16 that the messages coming from Jadotville were getting more desperate.

When O'Brien describes the news that Quinlan relayed of a request for a cease-fire by the Burgomaster of Jadotville, he says that he and the senior UN leadership in Katanga were "feeling very happy about Jadotville…I was pleased…because I thought it meant that the Africans in the gendarmerie were no longer willing to fight, or even act as a screen for the European enterprise."

O'Brien even adds that the Irish battalion commander, Lt. Col. Hugh McNamee, was content about the situation and had briefed the newly arrived Irish Minister for External Affairs, Frank Aiken, saying, "Situation well under control in Jadotville. No serious casualties. Five other ranks slightly wounded, some of them with shell shock. A truce was asked for last afternoon by Lord Mayor. Conditions very acceptable to Irish. Company Commander invited by Chief of Police to tour town today."

The next message O'Brien refers to is one from the early hours of Sunday morning, "0500 hours—A Company completely surrounded at Jadotville, estimated enemy at two thousand. Running short of food and water."

Another message relayed to O'Brien the severity of A Company's position since the cease-fire, "Position very acute. Despite promises still no water made available. Very severe pressure being exerted on them [A Company]."

Word came through at 1935 hours on Sunday evening that the garrison had formally surrendered.

O'Brien poses the question, "What had happened on the Saturday afternoon and how had it been reversed during Saturday night?"

Essentially, what had happened was, having failed to out-fight A Company, the Katangans had out-foxed them, and indeed the ONUC leadership in Katanga.

When Comdt. Quinlan was summoned to a meeting on Saturday night by a Major Makita and told he would have to give up his main weaponry and move locations as part of the cease-fire arrangement, he knew his position was untenable.

Agreeing to the cease-fire in one sense had been a mistake. It gave the initiative back to the Katangans, who had suffered a bad mauling in their last attack on the Irish positions. As already mentioned, so demoralized were the native troops that the mercenary officers were actually shooting their own men to stop a complete rout occurring.

O'Brien states that the UN was remiss in trying to communicate with and galvanize these "potential mutineers" around Jadotville. He asserts that there were also many native gendarmerie officers who "rejected the authority of foreign officers illegally present in Katanga."

In other words, according to O'Brien, the UN had failed to communicate to potential allies that they were on the same side. Apparently attempts to do this by radio broadcasts on September 14 resulted in "a stinging rebuke for our 'propaganda' and an order to confine ourselves…to objective news bulletins…It was clear our exhortations had to stop."

Had Quinlan even been made aware of the state of poor morale of the forces ranged against him, he could have made a different estimate of the situation.

Instead, while UN officials and the Irish battalion thought everything was rosy in the Jadotville garden with the initial news of the truce, it was really the end of resistance.

Getting Quinlan to agree to a truce was just the first step to luring the Irish troops by stealth into the surrender the Katangan soldiers had earlier failed to win on the field of battle.

However, one cannot hold Quinlan to account for this in any way, as he was still trying to make decisions based on incorrect information coming to him from Battalion HQ.

In fairness to HQ, this was undoubtedly coming from higher authority, but incorrect information is absolutely no substitute for good intelligence for the commander on the ground.

In some cases, erroneous information had completely undermined Quinlan's negotiating position. On the Saturday after the request by Major Makita for the Irish to store all their weapons at the one location, Quinlan correctly came to the conclusion that the Katangans had no intention of keeping their cease-fire agreement, but would just erode it bit by bit.

Quinlan was acutely aware of Katangan forces that had moved closer to his position in violation of the cease-fire: there was also a company of paracommandos now deployed to his rear.

When Quinlan notified his HQ of these changes, they cautioned him to hang on and to inform the Katangans that UN jets were on the way.

"I was instructed to tell the Burgomaster that UN jets would be over Jadotville if they attempted anything. I asked that these jets be sent over as soon as possible as a show of force. When I informed the enemy of UN jets, they wilted visibly.

"Nevertheless, they now became more harsh in their demands and now insisted we move to a hotel in town. There was still no question of surrender."

Despite requests, the water was still not turned on. It becomes obvious now that the Katangans were trying all in their power to denude A Company of their fighting capacity and maneuver them into a situation where they would have no alternative but to surrender.

However, the Katangans also knew they didn't have much time. If UN airpower arrived, the fight would be up and the opportunity for 150 UN hostages would have flown.

On Sunday at noon, just after the Fouga jet, supposed to be grounded as part of the cease-fire terms, had swooped over the Irish positions in a show of force, Quinlan was summoned to Jadotville town for high-level talks.

This time the ante had been upped considerably. Facing Quinlan when he arrived at the hotel chosen for negotiations was none other than Godefroid Munongo, Minister of the Interior for Katanga, and reputed killer of Patrice Lumumba.

But when he faced Quinlan, he had no bayonet drawn to thrust into the Kerryman's chest—just an outstretched hand. He smilingly congratulated the Irish officer on his men's stand and their soldierly qualities.

However, he admonished the UN in general and particularly singled out the Indian contingent who were reputed to have murdered Katangan prisoners they had taken during the Elisabethville fighting.

Therefore, he said, A Company must now surrender. They had fought bravely, but he couldn't hold back the troops that were now massing any longer.

In agreeing to the earlier cease-fire, the Irish had given much and received little, not even the water they had been promised. But then none of this had seemed likely, even to O'Brien and Lt. Col. McNamee who had seemed so delighted earlier with the terms of the Irish truce.

The Katangans had simply used the UN's lack of focus and will to apply military methodology against itself—a piece of classic asymmetrical warfare, long before Al-Qaeda had even reared its head.

No UN jets arrived. This was another fine example of going to war, UN style.

First, the UN engaged in indecision as to whether it's a war footing to stop a province seceding or a police action. Then, it engaged in actions that its forces were plainly not equipped for.

Why wasn't air support sought in the early stages of the planning of Operation Morthor? One jet could have made the difference for Quinlan and his men. Having said that, one series of well-aimed radio broadcasts at the native population in the Jadotville area could also have done so.

Instead, it is obvious that neither O'Brien nor the various military officers running operations had any grasp of the gravity of Quinlan's situation. Had they been studying his radio traffic, the news of the surrender should not have been at all surprising. The bluff about the jets just hurried it along.

Quinlan returned to his company and called an officer's conference to discuss this new ultimatum. His officers, particularly the young platoon commanders, were aghast and wanted to fight on if at all possible.

Lt. Carey gives a flavor of the tension that must have been in the room as the Irish officers contemplated the unthinkable:

I voiced my views in the strongest terms and did not believe we would surrender. [Lt.] Tom Quinlan felt the same and so did Joe Leech and Liam Donnelly. As Tom and myself were single it was easier for us to make that decision. It was, however, a dreadful decision for the married officers.

But when it came right down to it, A Company no longer even had the meager means they started with to defend themselves any longer. Lt. Kevin Knightly's armored cars had been an essential part of the defense, and now the locks for his Vickers machine guns were kaput. Without them, the weapons couldn't function correctly. Knightly and his cavalry corps men had fought valiantly throughout and had fired well over fifteen thousand machine-gun rounds in defense of their comrades. The lack of such firepower for a future defense would be disastrous.

An attempt at a breakout would also have been a disaster, considering the fact that all the motorized transport had been destroyed by the Fouga's bombing runs.

Carey, Knightly, and Donnelly were by far the most determined to fight on. They are to be commended for their fighting spirit, in the finest traditions of the Irish soldier. But had they been given their heads by Quinlan, they and their men would certainly have been needlessly slaughtered.

Once the practicalities had been thrashed out and the other officers had finished their frank exchanges on the merits and demerits of surrender, Quinlan alone made the final decision. He returned to tell Munongo that he would agree to his terms.

By doing this, Quinlan gave the Katangan regime over 150 hostages. But if he had fought on and his men were massacred, it would have been nearly impossible to have prevented blood-letting on a mass scale. The province would have been plunged into a complete war of attrition. It would have been very difficult for UN military planners to have avoided a tit-for-tat situation arising.

Quinlan gave orders for the support weapons and other equipment to be destroyed and all documents to be burned. He then went to inform Battalion HQ by radio.

In one message (it's not clear whether this was before or after meeting Munongo, but it is more likely it was after) Quinlan says, "Require decision from Aiken." Here Quinlan is looking for the highest governmental authority available to be made aware of the situation, and no decision has been made yet about surrender. It seems Quinlan was stalling the decision for as long as he could.

HQ replied, saying, "Proud of your gallant stand. You are constantly in our prayers and thoughts."

Then, according to Sgt. Walter Hegarty, who was present in Company HQ when the messages were being sent, the following happened. A message was sent to Gen. McKeown, saying, "We have *not* surrendered."

The reply was, "General McKeown has your message."

Then from Jadotville to Elisabethville, "We have our arms but no food."

The reply to this one was, "God Bless you."

Then, Jadotville, "If you want us to hold out, OK, but take the bridge."

It is not clear what the message that had been sent from Elisabethville was, but it was one of the last and would have been informing them that A Company were accepting the surrender terms.

The following reply is agreed to have happened, in particular by Sgt. Hegarty and Lt. Carey. According to Carey:

He informed HQ of his intentions and received a return message: "*An bhfuil tú ag tryregint na bhfear* [Are you deserting the men]?" This was a dreadful slur on the integrity of an outstanding commander, courageous and brave, and was like a slap in the face and the final indignity to an outstanding leader.

It does seem odd that with all the earlier praiseworthy messages, someone would now attempt to goad Quinlan at a time when his future was, to say the least, uncertain.

There have been numerous conspiracy theories, dating back to old feuds which had arisen at an officer's mess function one St Patrick's night many years ago.

However, it is possible that the translation got screwed up. While the Irish Army regularly use Irish to transmit voice messages by radio during operational situations, there are few who are native speakers in the Army.

When researching this part of the book, I asked an accomplished native speaker to translate the phrase from English into Irish and got: "*An bhfuil tú ag threighe doch chuid fir?*" It is conceivable the message got garbled, either in the transmission or interpretation.

However, if not, it was an unpardonable act considering the weight Quinlan must have felt on his shoulders concerning his men's safety when they would be in captivity.

Had Quinlan been given direct orders to follow one or other course of action, he would have willingly carried them out. Had he been told to fight on, he most certainly would have, as would his men. But directions from Elisabethville were vague at best and most information, such as that about the jet, erroneous.

No one seemed to have a full picture at the top of the chain of command and no one seemed to be willing to take a definite decision.

As Walter Hegarty put it, "Not one word to guide him, no statement of what was required. They had left him on the cross…No matter what he did now, someone would say it was wrong."

Although Quinlan insisted on written terms of surrender regarding the location they were to be held in and that they would be allowed to hold their small arms, all these terms would be broken by the Katangans.

Here follows a transcript of the original surrender document. Quinlan signs off in Irish as Patrick S. Quinlan Commandant, Officer Commanding A Company, 35th Battalion, ONUC:

Jadotville

17 September 1961

I, Comdt. Patrick Quinlan, Officer Commanding the United Nations troops in Jadotville, hereby agree to the terms of surrender of Minister Munongo because the Irish force is here in a peaceful role and any further action will result in the loss of African and Irish lives.

I also wish to state that my troops fought only in self-defense having been fired on while attending Mass the morning of 13 Sept, 1961 at 0740 hours. It is also agreed that the Irish forces will have their arms stored at the location of the Irish troops' accommodation.

In the absence of orders from higher authority, I take the responsibility for this decision.

Signed:

Padraig S Ó Caoindealbháin Ceannfort
Oifigeach i gceannais Complucht A
35 Cathlán ONUC

Godefroid Munongo
Ministre L'Intérieur
Katanga

Demonstrating an efficacy of information dissemination that was beyond the UN at the time, the Katangans lost no time getting the news of the Irish surrender out to their sympathizers in Europe and the United States.

On Monday morning, Ireland woke up to the stomach-churning news that 157 of her sons were in deep peril, if not dead.

The *Irish Independent* ran with the banner headline, "Jadotville Post Overrun," and underneath carried it on with "Beleaguered Irish Company again Attacked. Casualties as UN Relieving Column Meets Big Force."

Previously, there had been headlines proclaiming that there were fifty or more deaths amongst the Irish troops. The country was glued to the BBC World Service and all of the newspapers.

Of course, the Katangan Ministry of Information played everyone perfectly. The country was in a furor and the Irish government couldn't get a straight answer out of the UN leadership. So it was prior to the actual fall of Jadotville that Minister for External Affairs Frank Aiken was dispatched to try and sort out reality from propaganda.

On Monday night, Gen. McKeown contacted Dublin with the following message:

It now appears that the garrison at Jadotville has been overwhelmed by vastly superior numbers.

The Company has acquitted itself well during the week in a difficult situation. It has become almost impossible to supply it with food and water not to mention the difficulty of getting reinforcements to it. In fact the strong two-company group, supported by four armored cars, incurred four killed, six missing, and twelve wounded in attempting to get through to them yesterday.

After the decision to accept Munongo's surrender terms, which meant moving to a disused hotel in Jadotville, Lts. Leech, Carey, and Donnelly had considered trying for a breakout that night with some of their men.

Their initial ardor had cooled when they considered the impracticalities—no transport, food, or water; fatigued soldiers; and sixty or so miles to be covered in unfamiliar bush terrain to reach Elisabethville, assuming they weren't ambushed like Force Kane Two.

Furthermore, they reasoned, it would have been disloyal to have left Quinlan and their comrades behind. However, that night was a tough one for Carey and his brother officers:

The second memory I have is of Tom Quinlan and myself in our room looking out at Jadotville and having such a dreadful feeling that after all the fighting we had surrendered and the feeling that as Irish officers we had let the Army, nation, and our families down.

It is now impossible to explain the feeling and I recall Tom Quinlan crying openly at the humiliation of it all. I wished I could cry but I just felt numb.

The rank-and-file had not been told, in an attempt to keep morale stable.

The next morning A Company paraded, stacked their weapons, and marched to captivity. Many of the younger soldiers had no idea they had surrendered.

There was every reason for the troops to feel concerned about how the natives would treat them as prisoners.

Sgt. Hegarty recorded how during the fighting there were regular phone calls to the Company HQ that a mob would be unleashed and the Irish troops would be eaten alive, to which Quinlan is reputed to have replied, "Well, I hope we don't give you indigestion."

Apparently, on the Friday night after the phone calls and during an easing off in the fighting, the native gendarmes had started roaring at the Irish lines, "Kill! Kill! Kill! Choppy-chop, choppy-chop [meaning, 'We will eat you']!"

Hegarty says that the only effect this had on the Irish troops was that "our lads replied with everything they'd got. When they stopped there were howls of agony and pain from the gends' lines. For the remainder of the night there was wholesale firing on both sides."

But now the shoe would be on the other foot. Some of the men guarding A Company would undoubtedly have had comrades killed during the days of fighting.

After having been marched away from their weapons and defensive positions, A Company were taken to a musty old hotel in Jadotville town. They were supplied with basic materials for their cooks to prepare as meals.

It wasn't necessarily going to be like surrendering to the Germans at Dunkirk and being led away to sit out the war in a prison camp with your Red Cross parcels. The very fact that the whole affair in Katanga was classified as neither war-fighting nor peacekeeping meant the normal rules didn't necessarily apply.

But while the younger soldiers had no initial idea of the gravity of the situation, the officers and older NCOs were expecting anything to happen. This was Africa after all, and horrible things had already happened to others in the Congo.

For Carey, the biggest problem was not knowing what was in store:

I felt dreadful tension for the first two weeks, not knowing what was to happen to us and expecting every day that some of us would be taken out and executed. My main concern was that I would be tortured and mutilated as we had heard had happened to troops in the past. I was also concerned that I would bear up in front of my platoon.

These were terrifying times for those officers who were fully informed. On previous occasions, UN troops had been found castrated and horribly mutilated.

On arrival at the hotel, Quinlan insisted that a routine be established to keep the men occupied. He ordered that regular PE lessons, including unarmed combat, be conducted. But this was soon stopped by their captors. He gave an order to fill all available bottles with petrol from their field cookers to make Molotov cocktails in case of an attempt to massacre them by the Katangans.

Lt. Carey had managed to hide a personal radio in a sack of rice in CQMS Pat Neville's stores and each night he would join Neville and storeman, Pte. Jack O'Brien, to listen clandestinely to the BBC World Service.

Quinlan would then be informed of any news that could be of use to him when he would meet with Katangan officials. Initially, A Company were well treated and guarded by Belgian and French mercenaries who showed them a healthy respect. Quinlan even managed to strike up a good relationship with an officer in charge of the guard detail.

But there were some tense times ahead for the Irish captives, who were now in a situation for which no soldier can ever really be trained or psychologically equipped.

The establishment of a routine by Quinlan was an essential tool in staving off the awful boredom and tedium for men that had, up until recently, been living on adrenaline. Without this and the continued leadership by NCOs and officers, discipline could easily have broken down.

There were a few hasty gibes made at one stage between troops who had been in the forward trenches and those who had been back at the Purfina garage villas during the mortar bombardments.

However, unit cohesion remained and the camaraderie built in combat was sustained. The other useful point about establishing a routine was that it kept the men's minds off what might happen to them. The older soldiers and the officers knew there was a real possibility of reprisals occurring.

After becoming captive, the Irish were joined by some other troops. Some were Irish soldiers, such as Comdt. Cahalane and his men, captured during fighting at Elisabethville. There was also a party of Italian medics also captured during.

In conversations with Quinlan, some of the European officers enquired as to his losses. When they heard there were only five wounded, they would not believe him. In fact, members of the gendarmerie were set to work digging up the Irish positions to find where the Irish had secreted their dead.

The result of this was to increase worries of reprisals to make the Irish pay for the death they had wrought on the Katangan forces. So when a Land Rover with a coffin on the back drew up outside the hotel where A Company were being held, tensions rose immeasurably. Was there going to be a killing?

It turned out the coffin was already filled and en route for burial. The driver had only stopped for a Katangan flag to be draped over it for the burial service. It was the body of one of the more senior mercenary officers, who had died of his wounds.

Another day, the troops were ordered to assemble on the hotel veranda. Quinlan, fearing the long-awaited reprisal, had some of the officers stay on the top balcony with the improvised petrol-bombs in case of an attack on the unarmed men.

Instead, after the men assembled, a press photographer arrived and took some shots. At the time, though they didn't know it, A Company was quite safe. President Tshombe wasn't about to let anything happen to his new propaganda prizes.

The week after surrendering, the Irish troops were graced with a visit by Tshombe himself. The Katangan President wanted to wring all he could from the UN now that he had so many of their troops as hostages.

Maximum propaganda was generated from the fact that they were being well treated. Lt. Carey and other officers noticed how the visit of Tshombe and earlier of Col. Muké of the gendarmerie had been quietly choreographed by white mercenary officers in the background.

This propaganda coup was enhanced by claims made by Katangans on the world stage that prisoners taken by members of the Indian UN contingent had been mistreated. The UN dismissed claims that any had been murdered in captivity by the Indians.

However, press reports that the Indians had killed twenty Katangan prisoners with grenades were later confirmed by Irish officers operating alongside them.

Years later, Lt. Joe Leech, now a colonel, confirmed these Indian atrocities to Col. J. T. O'Neill in an interview for a paper he was preparing for a peacekeeping journal.

It must be said that the Indians had suffered too, with a number of their troops having been abducted and shot in cold blood, including a young Sikh major who after abduction was never seen again. Wars are grisly affairs, even ones carried out under blue flags.

A Company were wheeled out for the international press corps to see, with a number of Irish journalists including Raymond Smith from the *Irish Independent* and John Ross from RTE.

There was also an English journalist named Peter Younghusband of the *Daily Mail*. Younghusband was a man who had earned the respect of Irish soldiers previously during his coverage of Congo affairs. He further endeared himself to the men of A Company when he agreed to take a package of mail and see that it was posted back to Ireland.

There are a number of contentious recollections regarding the mail and journalists. CQMS Pat Neville alleges that another journalist had been asked to take the mail bag, but had refused, and an argument had started. Younghusband, on hearing the commotion, came over and took the bag, simply saying, "'I'll look after that, CQMS.' There was no fuss and he did—all that post got home and gave great comfort to our families."

The men had only been able to send one short Red Cross postcard home to their families to tell them they were still alive since becoming captive.

Comdt. Quinlan says he gave a letter containing some of the pages he had saved from the company radio log to RTE journalist John Ross and asked him to post them home. Undoubtedly, these pages would have referred to where Quinlan asked for clarification about orders concerning surrender, and most likely would have included the exchange where he appeared to be accused of deserting his men.

Apparently, Ross mentioned the package when he was back at Battalion HQ and was told that they would look after it. Nothing was seen of it again.

Much has been made of this by veterans of A Company. If it did refer to the remark about deserting his men, perhaps someone who spoke in haste, or realized the message had been misunderstood, decided to give the log pages a decent burial. In any event, Quinlan himself never commented in public about it or engaged in any formal or legal proceedings when the Jadotville episode ended.

Following Tshombe's visit, the guard was changed and the Irish found themselves under a much more austere regime. Then, over his clandestine radio, Lt. Carey learned that UN Secretary-General Dag

Hammarskjöld had been killed in an airplane crash. The UN leader had been en route to a peace conference in Northern Rhodesia with the Katangan leadership.

To this day there is speculation about the nature of Hammarskjöld's death. Was it an accident, or was he killed to enable the Katangan secession to succeed?

Whatever its cause, from A Company's point of view it was a setback. They had felt sure they would be released as part of conditions for negotiations. What they didn't realize was they were an ace in the pack for the Katangans to get conditions favorable for negotiation.

Within days of Hammarskjöld's death and after three weeks of captivity in Jadotville, A Company were ordered to get ready to move. The troops were separated into their platoons, loaded onto buses and taken west, away from Elisabethville to the Katangan stronghold of Kolwezi.

This move seemed to augur badly for the Irish. After an hour their buses wheeled off the road and into a native township.

"Suddenly the villagers gathered around us, waving, gesticulating all sort of threats should they get their hands on us," remembers Lt. Noel Carey.

The village Lt. Carey and his men had been driven into had lost many of its menfolk at Jadotville. At one stage the crowd had started throwing clods of dirt at the buses and the Irish were sure they would be dragged out and torn apart.

This was another fine example of Katangan Psyops. The Irish were reminded that attempting to escape in this region, where the natives had lost heavily fighting against them, would be suicide. It was a shaken company of troops that arrived at their final destination in Kolwezi that night. But their ordeal was not yet over. As the men debussed, a search far more thorough than at Jadotville was instituted.

Lt. Carey says, "As the first group dismounted from the bus

we could hear loud roaring and some of the lads being struck and kicked around."

What Lt. Carey and the rest of the troops soon learned was that anyone discovered with bayonets or any form of ammunition was being subjected to a merciless beating by the native Katangan guards.

For Carey, the proud young officer who had not wanted to surrender at all, it was an experience he'd rather forget. "We were individually searched, a most humiliating experience."

There were no sympathetic white mercenaries in attendance now. Anything could happen. Any pretense at respect was now dispensed with and the Irish were instructed to strip off their boots and socks, and open up and lay out all their personal effects for a full examination.

"There was a panic on our bus," recalls Carey. "A few of my platoon found ammunition and grenades in their rucksacks. I took them and as the guards had dismounted from our bus, I was able to stuff them down the back seat."

For Quinlan, to see his men being abused like this was the ultimate humiliation. Men such as Pte. John Gorman recalled that he went

white as a sheet, and his jaw clamped shut like a steel trap. When the gend officer was lashing out, Quinlan's eyes seemed to go on fire. Then, just as things were really getting out of hand, he elbowed his way through the armed Katangan soldiers and demanded to see their CO.

They got a shock and seemed half afraid of him, even though they all had their rifles pointed at him and he with one hand as long as the other. When some officer showed up, Quinlan lashed him out of it like he was a young recruit on the parade ground in Custume Barracks. He threatened to report him to everyone from Tshombe to the bloody Pope!

For the stoic Walter Hegarty, there was always someone worse off than he:

> We turned back to land in a large building in Kolwezi with barbed wire and heavily guarded…while a little pig of a Katangan officer called us the "Beasts of L'ONU" in French.

> Next order was to take off our berets, then the dear fellow gave an impassioned speech to his satellites on how the murderers should be treated with a demo. The poor soldiers were pointing rifles at us till we left.

The next day Comdt. Quinlan was up and at 'em again, demanding to see higher authority about better conditions for his men. One of the few things he managed to get, much to Lt. Carey's delight, was Rhodesian cream butter. After six months without real butter, it would be the only treat A Company would get in captivity.

Two weeks later the troops were ordered to have packed and be ready to move at first light the next morning. When they swung out of Kolwezi, A Company had no idea where they were going. What they didn't know was that stringent negotiations were going on for their release, and the fine details were being hammered out about a prisoner exchange as all hostilities had now been suspended.

As the buses drove through the midday heat, with armed guards within and atop the buses, the natives came out to shout abuse at them. The Irish just sat and suffered through the heat without food or water.

Soon they were passing Jadotville and their old position and over Lufira bridge and on to Camp Massart, the gendarmerie camp in Elisabethville. Here the troops were held for the next number of hours as negotiations continued.

The camp was bursting with mercenaries, armed settlers, and

gendarmes. The mood was distinctly hostile—so much so that the A Company men preferred to squeeze their bladders and stay aboard the bus rather than brave the gauntlet of abuse some of their comrades suffered when being escorted to the toilet.

Then at 1700 hours the buses were off, speeding along the suburbs of Elisabethville. Lt. Carey thought they were on their way out of captivity, but he suddenly realized, "We were actually traveling back the way we had come this morning. We were shattered as we crossed the Lufira bridge."

Interestingly, also joining A Company at this time were the ubiquitous Charles Kearney and his Scottish pal Hamish Mathieson.

Kearney and Mathieson went to Elisabethville and UN jurisdiction where they had agreed to accompany three Irish officers on a reconnaissance mission of the gendarmerie HQ.

Kearney, Mathieson, Capt. Mick Purfield (later to be decorated with a DSM), Capt. Terry McKeever, and Capt. Mark Carroll, who had been in the thick of the action at Lufira, were captured while making their approach by car on a road adjacent to the camp.

They were threatened with execution the next day, but were saved by an order from President Tshombe, who didn't want Katanga's public image damaged. Following this order, the men were held with the rest of A Company.

Kearney had been working as a technician with Union Minière when the conflict unraveled. He told Quinlan how he and his friends had resigned from the company when it was plainly obvious they were financing and supporting the Katangan attacks on the UN forces.

The last straw for Kearney had been the day he saw JCBs being turned into armored vehicles to defend Lufira bridge against the Irish-led Force Kane. He had also been urged to join the rest of the white population in fighting A Company at Jadotville.

The notion of taking up arms against his countrymen was out

of the question for Kearney, so he fed them information as best he could. His final estimate was that there were between four thousand and five thousand Katangans ranged against the Irish, but that only the white mercenaries really wanted to fight.

He also estimated that A Company had accounted for the deaths of up to three hundred of the gendarmerie, including up to thirty or more mercenary officers. This judgement was made based on the number of coffins being brought into the area for the dead. Apparently only the whites merited a coffin.

After another two weeks, Quinlan received word to have his men ready to move again. Quinlan did this and also decided that this time, wherever he and his men were going, they weren't coming back.

He gave word to his officers and selected NCOs who were going to try and take over their buses when they stopped. The selection was important because the officers and men were to be separated. Walter Hegarty was one of those selected:

> I had unarmed combat training from having done my Physical Training Instructor course. I was told to prepare another soldier to help me and to be ready on Quinlan's signal to overpower the armed guard at the front of the bus.
>
> Men were dotted around the bus with orders to jump the guards. Then we would take over the bus and drive like hell for the Indian roadblock on the edge of Elisabethville.

The reason for driving "like hell" was to knock their Katangan guards, armed with machine guns, off the roof.

But when the buses hit Elisabethville, it wasn't to Camp Massart they drove, but to an old disused airport. As the buses entered the gates, the captive Irish spotted the vehicles with UN livery. A shout went up and they disembarked out of captivity and back into UN hands.

It was 1620 hours on October 26, 1961, and the siege at Jadot-ville was now finally over.

14

AFTERMATH AND PAYBACK

War is something no adventurous man should miss ...
and only a fool will try twice.

—Ernest Hemingway

What became known as the Second Battle of Katanga broke out on December 5, 1961.

There is some dispute as to whether the UN manufactured a pretext to finally finish the job it started with Operation Morthor, or whether the Katangans provoked the UN by taking over the road into the airport to stymie UN resupply operations.

In his book *The New Mercenaries* Anthony Mockler claims, "The keepers of the world's conscience seemed to have no more scruples than any war-mongering nation state in seizing on the flimsiest of pretexts as an excuse for launching an attack."

He believes the next stage of combat was precipitated by a document that fell into UN hands showing how the defense of Katanga would be conducted by dividing the province into five military zones under white mercenary leadership.

When hostilities broke out anew on December 5, the UN had

acquired significant air assets from India, Ethiopia, and Sweden. Round Two kicked off with a crushing air raid on the Katangans' airbase at Kolwezi.

Jacques Delen's Fouga, which had done so much damage at Jadotville, Lufira, and Elisabethville, was finally destroyed by the Canberra bombers of the Indian air force. However, the mercenary-led forces put up fierce resistance and continued to be aided by the local population, both black and white.

The Irish 35th Battalion were now joined by the 36th, fresh out from Ireland. Both units were to be directly involved in this campaign at the Battle of the Tunnel, as indeed were elements of the rearmed A Company.

Lt. Carey and Capt. Donnelly had landed the privilege of leading fifty-eight members of A Company onto one of the Globemasters, flying back to Ireland on November 28. The rest of A Company was to get another crack at the gends before heading home.

The 35th was supposed to be replaced by the 36th, but the new outbreak of hostilities meant using all available troops. One of the first actions of what became the Second Battle of Katanga was the clearing of Katangan roadblocks at the old runway in Elisabethville.

On December 5, what was left of A Company spearheaded the attack on the two companies of gendarmes waiting for them behind the barricades.

The new UN Secretary-General, U Thant, had given full and unambiguous authority for the UN forces to pursue all ground and air action to restore freedom of movement in Elisabethville area.

Brigadier K. A. S. Raja was now in command of all UN military operations in Katanga. He ordered an Irish-Gurkha combined infantry company with Irish and Swedish armor rolled on up "Charlie Route" to smash open the airport road.

Comdt. Falques and his Algerian war veterans, however, were not giving up Katanga without a fight. Despite having lost their edge in the airpower stakes, the mercenaries and native Katangan soldiers fought well, utilizing mortar, machine-gun, and sniper fire to inflict casualties on the UN troops.

The attack briefly faltered when the Indian officer leading the assault was mown down with seven of his Gurkhas in a hail of machine-gun fire. Capt. Art Magennis had to take control of the overall operation, communicating with the feisty Gurkhas by sign language.

The little fighters from Nepal needed no great urging anyway, being only too anxious to avenge the deaths of their comrades.

The A Company men, mostly of No. 2 Platoon under Lt. Tom Quinlan and Platoon Sgt. Walter Hegarty, were given the difficult job of winkling out the snipers shooting up the flanks of the attacking UN column. This they did without compunction, inflicting maximum casualties and managing not to lose any men themselves.

Because of the death of the Indian OC, Capt. Magennis decided to switch the direction of the attack. But first he needed to find the extreme part of the enemy's left flank.

Not content with nearly being shredded with shrapnel at Jadot-ville, Sgt. Hegarty piped up. "I'll find it," he declared, and set off with two of his men as they came under a hail of fire.

Having exactly located the position, the final attack was begun with the A Company men at the vanguard. In a dogged assault they drove the attackers away from the airstrip in disarray.

Comdt. Quinlan's men were to find themselves in combat again, literally days before they boarded the Globemasters to go home.

This time it was on the night of December 12, when the Katangans set up a roadblock near the Soco petrol depot in order to secure fuel supplies for themselves and to cut off the Irish and Swedish camps from the UN Headquarters in Elisabethville.

Comdt. Quinlan mobilized A Company once more, led them through the defensive fire and penetrated right into the depot. Taking maximum advantage of the confusion caused by the darkness of night and explosions from their antitank guns, the men of Lt. Tom Quinlan's No. 2 Platoon set the much-needed depot ablaze in an angry glow that could be seen up to twent-five miles away.

This was A Company's parting shot in what can rightly be called the Katangan War. Quinlan had a grin on his face as he surveyed the gends running around amidst the explosions at Soco.

"See what we can do, given half a chance?" he mused.

The battle juddered along until December 21, with the mercenaries putting up a spirited resistance. But the UN was learning their lessons in war, and their superior numbers along with their fire and air superiority won out. Comdt. Falques quit the fight thereafter, vowing never to take orders again from an African leader.

However, there would ultimately be a Third Battle of Katanga between December 28, 1962 and January 21, 1963. This time the UN, now having upwards of ten thousand troops at its disposal, gave an ultimatum to President Tshombe to end secession.

This was rejected and ONUC moved with overwhelming force to occupy the main towns and cities of Katanga. This time there was only token resistance. By now the mercenary reins of leadership had been taken up by the infamous ex-French marine, Bob Denard. With ONUC hot on their heels, he and his mercenaries scuttled across the border to Angola. So ended the Katangan secession.

Unfortunately for the Congo, this did not herald peace. Instead, what became known as the Simba uprising began in 1964. It led to a new influx of white mercenaries, this time under Irishman "Mad Mike" Hoare. Many Europeans and Africans were to die in the blood-letting.

But before writing off the UN's Congo adventure for not stabilizing the country or bringing peace, one thing should be remembered. One of the prime objectives of UN intervention was to prevent the Congo becoming a Cold War battlefield, and in that it prevailed.

Just in time to celebrate the Christmas of 1961, the entirety of

A Company, with Quinlan at their head, arrived to a tumultuous reception in Athlone. As the troops returned to Custume Barracks, the families and friends of men that had been feared dead feted Quinlan as the hero of the hour with a torchlight procession through the town.

But very quickly afterwards, the whole event faded almost entirely from public consciousness. Considering the huge print and broadcast media coverage, it seems unbelievable that such an event simply slunk out of the public arena.

Both Sgt. Hegarty and Lt. Tom Quinlan would later be decorated for their actions with Distinguished Service Medals. The DSM is second only to the Military Medal for Gallantry (MMG) in the list of valor decorations in the Irish Defense Forces.

Lt. Quinlan's DSM citation read:

For distinguished service with the United Nations Force in the Republic of the Congo, for leadership during the period September to December 1961, in Katanga…His platoon engaged in action on a number of occasions and displayed aggressiveness and spirit of a high degree, which was due to his excellent qualities of leadership and courage.

The following was cited for Sgt. Hegarty:

For distinguished service with the United Nations Force in the Republic of the Congo, during two service periods in 1960 and 1961. He displayed outstanding leadership, resourcefulness, and courage on numerous occasions. His personal example and efficiency were an inspiration to others and a boost to the morale of his men.

However, the issue of decorations was to become a bone of contention in its own right regarding Jadotville. As far as the veterans of A Company are concerned, there were no decorations awarded for acts of valor that took place during the action there.

This was despite Comdt. Quinlan making a lengthy list of recommendations for many of his men who performed as outstanding soldiers and leaders in the face of enemy fire.

Some in the Army felt that Sgt. Hegarty and Lt. Quinlan's awards were for acts that covered Jadotville, but were not specific to it. Despite the two soldier's citations including a time span that broadly included Jadotville, they never specifically mention the siege.

Many excuses have been given for this. One of the most plausible is that the DSM did not exist as a decoration in 1961, and that Comdt. Quinlan had simply recommended too many of his men for the MMG. Senior military sources maintained that the problem was whether to award one or none under such circumstances.

However, it does seem distinctly odd that the actions taken under severe fire such as that of CQMS Pat Neville and Cpl. William "Bob" Allen when, in helping Lt. Hovden's helicopter land, did not merit a decoration.

Yet the same Cpl. Allen was to be decorated with a DSM for displaying and inspiring "leadership and courage...by his personal example...in numerous engagements supporting Indian and Ethiopian troops...in December 1962 and January 1963."

One can't help wondering what Cpl. Allen did in 1962 and 1963 that stood out more than his actions at Jadotville.

Considering that there was no action taken on a number of other Jadotville recommendations, it does cause one to raise an eyebrow slightly to learn that Cpl. John Kavanagh was rightly decorated for his courage at Lufira bridge on September 16, 1961.

Cpl. Kavanagh, part of the unfortunate Force Kane Two, left the protection of an armored car to rescue a member of his unit pinned down by enemy fire.

While there were many recommendations for decorations at

Jadotville, here follows an example of one. This verbatim example is taken directly from the "Recommendations for Recognition for Meritorious Service" for Lt. Noel Carey. It was originally made by his platoon sergeant, Sgt. Kevin McLoughlin:

> The exceedingly high morale of the platoon was mostly due to his easy unassuming approach and courageous devotion to duty. Lt. Carey was evident at all times moving from position to position, even under heavy fire, encouraging and personally taking over and operating the Bren guns to give much needed relief to the gunners. On arrival of the helicopter which was under intense mortar and SA [Sustained Automatic] fire, by his coolness and quick appraisal of the situation, he immediately led the occupants of his trench to an alternative position and thereby avoided certain casualties as the helicopter landed approx. two feet from the vacated trench. On inspection some time afterwards, this position was found to be literally riddled by large caliber ammunition.

These sentiments were endorsed by Comdt. Quinlan, who described him as "a fearless officer with the qualities of leadership which are demanded in desperate situations such as this."

There certainly seemed to be anomalies in the way Jadotville was being perceived in the immediate aftermath and as the years progressed.

On Saturday, September 23, 1961, the *Daily Mail*, a paper not always associated with benevolent feelings to the Irish state, ran the headline, "The Tigers of Jadotville."

After his recent visit to see the captive A Company, the English journalist Younghusband wrote that having fought valiantly to defend their positions, "these justly proud Irishmen are now VIPs, very important prisoners of Katanga."

In writing this, Younghusband articulated two salient points of truth—firstly, that A Company had fulfilled their duty and had nothing to be ashamed of; and secondly, that their captivity was a major asset to the Katangans as leverage to grind the UN military machine to a halt, but also as propaganda to show the world how the supposed bullies of Tshombe really treated their prisoners.

Despite this, the rot was setting in. A Company had surrendered, and it didn't make the Irish feel good about themselves. It wasn't that the Irish Army needed to convince the world that Jadotville had been a considerable piece of defense against overwhelming odds. It was more that they needed to convince themselves.

As Lt. Carey and his comrades settled back into routine at "the farm," as the Irish Battalion HQ in Elisabethville was called, they began to sense an attitude of hostility amongst some of their comrades.

"However," says Carey, "after a honeymoon of a week, a well-earned rest, and being resupplied with weapons, a certain animosity began to develop between some members of the Battalion and A Company because of the surrender."

Irish Times journalist Cathal O'Shannon agrees that "there was a palpable sense of shame" within the Irish contingent after Jadotville.

This can only be explained by the Army's inexperience with overseas operations at the time and the sensitivities such inexperience can arouse.

In the years after Jadotville, there were those who spoke up about it. In the 1960s, former Army officer and Independent TD, Jack McQuillan, claimed there was a "bloodlust mentality in the country and the men would have been recognized as heroes if they had died. The conduct of the Irish troops and their officers at Jadotville deserves the highest commendation. They showed common sense, intelligence and integrity. Had they not displayed those characteristics, a further fifty or sixty young Irishmen might have been killed."

Fianna Fáil TD Lionel Booth also paid tribute to A Company

in the Dáil in 1963, "Everybody—officers, NCOs, and men—were [*sic*] magnificent and, when they were involved in further combat operations shortly after they had rejoined the main force, they showed that again."

Perhaps these politicians were aware that within the Army, the term "Jadotville Jack" was now a term of derision and one that was gaining creeping acceptance in other Army units.

In one incident in the Curragh some years after Jadotville, a major row broke out between troops from the Western Command, from which most of the soldiers who served at Jadotville had been drawn, and the Curragh troops.

Taunts had been exchanged in the canteen between the two groups, not an unusual occurrence in the times for young, fit red-blooded soldiers. However, such were feelings about Jadotville at the time in the Army that a small riot broke out. Belt buckles, boots, fists, broken furniture … anything went.

According to some who were there, were it not for the forceful response of the local Military Police contingent, there would have been serious injury. As it was, quite a number of troops involved had to be taken to hospital.

Even though the only formal statements made about the siege were respectful, acceptance of an attitude of shame towards Jadotville had sprouted in the Army and had been allowed to grow.

There is enough of a prima facie case to indicate that the Army felt embarrassed by Jadotville.

As Ireland continued to carve out a reputation as a country that could punch above its weight on missions such as the current ones in Liberia and Kosovo, its inexperience departed. But, like a shaky adolescent's first moment on stage, the Irish Army's Congo chapter broke new ground in its history. It is understandable then that they would want to have a clean slate.

It is also understandable that anything that would seem not to reflect well would be quietly consigned to the dusty shelf of history, as has been the case with so many other armies. But even this is not excusable in the case of Jadotville, for the simple reason that any faults and mistakes regarding the operation lie largely with an inept UN leadership vision for the whole ONUC operation.

The Irish officers and soldiers had not experienced anything like this before. Certainly, errors were made, but the essential thing was that they were made in good faith.

Perhaps as a result of this misplaced shame, there is very little about Jadotville in the history books, Irish and otherwise, yet it forms an integral part of the Congo story.

The fact is that the fall of Jadotville called a halt to any further fighting by the UN to attain the objectives set by Operation Morthor, namely the ending of the Katangan secession.

The failure of Operation Morthor gave heart to the Katangan forces and state which were riding high in the world's perception. It enabled them to present an image to the world of the underdog barking back and calling the bluff of the UN behemoth.

But because the story of Jadotville has not been properly chronicled, especially from the Irish perspective, a void had been left. Such a void demonstrates our national apathy at best, but at worst it meant that we as a nation have left a vacant space for others to cast slurs on our fighting men.

The passage below by Mockler is a case in point. He believes the Jadotville garrison should have attempted a breakout during one of the actions by Force Kane One and Two at Lufira. Mockler is scathing in his criticism of the conduct of UN forces in general during Operation Morthor. He is particularly dismissive of A Company's predicament:

> On 13 September United Nations Indian troops under Brigadier Raja seized control of key points in Elisabeth-

ville and throughout the state. Conor Cruise [O'Brien] announced unwisely: "Katanga's secession is ended." Next day the Katangese gendarmerie counterattacked. Heavy fighting followed in Elisabethville and elsewhere. Three days later the Irish garrison at Jadotville surrendered to the Katangese. Admittedly they were surrounded and their water supply had been cut off. But their position, although unpleasant, was not desperate; if their morale had been high they could have fought their way out and inflicted a crushing defeat on the Katangese and the mercenaries. The least that can be said is that this surrender was hardly in the spirit of Irish history.

There is a particular reason for including the above passage. At least Mockler has put his money where his mouth is and committed his opinions to paper. Many did not, blaming A Company for lacking fighting spirit in whispered asides in messes.

However, the foregoing chapters, I believe, explain in some detail why Mockler's assertions about Jadotville are completely wrong. Lack of support weapons, transport, and perhaps most vital of all, accurate intelligence on both the enemy's capability and morale, all prevented A Company from doing anything Mockler suggests they could have.

In addition, there was the small matter of the Fouga jet to consider and the mauling that had been handed out to Force Kane Two. Had Quinlan led his men on a breakout, already weary from lack of food, water, and sleep, many would surely have been slaughtered needlessly. Had he tried to fight on after his position had been undermined during the cease-fire, he would have subjected troops to wasteful deaths. Certainly accepting the cease-fire when A Company had won the firefight was a mistake, but it must be remembered that even higher authority couldn't furnish suitable strategic direction and seemed to be in agreement with the cease-fire terms.

The biggest "crime" Quinlan committed was to be outmaneuvered by the cease-fire. It would seem that the Katangans undermined his position bit by bit and played on the fact that his directions from higher up the chain of command were confused, as indeed was the case for most of Operation Morthor.

The biggest mistake the Army has made since this was to consider it a blot on their copy book and quietly to hope the incident would go away. If it was a blot on anybody's copy book, it was ultimately the UN's, because of its organization and strategy in implementing operations in the Congo.

The problems here began as far back as when Ralph Bunche arrived in the Congo and clashed with the professional military advice of his Force Commander, Gen. Carl von Horn. This was compounded by the fact that intelligence gathering and public perception management as tools of peacekeeping or enforcement were ignored.

Having UN Headquarters in New York influence operational decisions on the ground, as in the case of insisting on a troop deployment to Jadotville in contravention of Brigadier Raja's advice, didn't help matters either.

In any event, the men of A Company went on about their careers. While Comdt. Quinlan retired as a full colonel, he never served overseas again.

Lt. Noel Carey returned home to marry his beloved Angela and was later promoted to the rank of captain. But he always felt that Jadotville was not an event the Army seemed to want to remember. "I was conscious that Jadotville was being buried by the Army, that I was not to talk about it and that it would be better for my career to let it die."

Carey had no idea of his platoon sergeant's recommending him for a decoration until over forty years had elapsed and he was carrying out an interview for the Army's archives department. Carey subsequently left the Army, going on to a career in the private sector in Cork, but his questions about Jadotville still lingered.

CQMS Neville went back to his career at Custume Barracks, Athlone, retiring in the senior NCO rank of BQMS.

Sgt. Walter Hegarty returned to Dún Uí Mhaolíosa, better known as Mellows Barracks in Galway, where he resumed his career with the 1st (Irish-speaking) Battalion. Shortly after his return he was promoted to the senior NCO rank of company sergeant, but left the Army some years later to pursue a career in the emergency services. He subsequently retired as Senior Fire Officer with the Galway local authority. Had he stayed in the Army, this gifted soldier would undoubtedly have been commissioned from the ranks.

Pte. John Gorman resumed his career with the 6th Infantry Battalion in Athlone. He went on to attain NCO rank and served with the UN in Cyprus. Though a physical condition he later developed prevented him from further overseas service, he served his full twenty-one years and retired to pursue another career in household maintenance.

"There isn't a day goes by that I don't think of Jadotville and the men I was with, particularly Comdt. Quinlan." As a result, Gorman has been very active in veterans' affairs with his local branch of the Irish United Nations Veterans Association (IUNVA). He is particularly involved in managing welfare matters concerning his comrades from Jadotville days.

Now the wheel has come full circle. The men who served at Jadotville have broken their silence. After his experience in Army archives, Noel Carey urged former Capt. Liam Donnelly to check his own file. He too, he discovered, had been recommended for a decoration, only to have been refused by the medals board.

When Carey wrote to seek answers under the Freedom of Information Act he was told the relevant file "is lost and cannot be found." However, Donnelly did compile a submission to the Dáil in 2004 where they requested a reopening of the Jadotville file by both the political and military authorities.

Added to this was a groundswell of public interest drummed up single-handedly by John Gorman. He has been tireless in his efforts to interest and inform the media, both local and national, about this issue.

To date he has given countless interviews to print and broadcast media. No outlet is too big or too small for Gorman. Whether it's RTE, Sky News Ireland, or Midlands Radio 3, he has been steadily pushing the Jadotville story back under the noses of a previously indifferent public.

This agitation gradually gained momentum. In 2004, Athlone Urban District Council and Longford-Roscommon Fine Gael TD Denis Naughten backed the call for a complete reassessment of what happened at Jadotville.

"It seems that only one side of the story has come out until now. The accounts of people directly involved over the five days directly contradicts the official report of what happened and they should now be heard. These men were left for dead. They should be given the opportunity to get back their good name. A full inquiry should take place even to set the record straight," Mr. Naughten said.

Then something gave. The former Defense Minister Michael Smith announced that the request from Athlone UDC for the men to be honored was "presently under examination."

Since then, in the earlier part of 2005, the newly incumbent Minister for Defense, Mr. Willie O'Dea, announced that an internal reexamination of the events surrounding Jadotville completely exonerated A Company and Comdt. Quinlan from any notion of unsoldierly behavior.

In March of 2005, Mr. O'Dea stated:

As outlined to the House on 26 January 2005, detailed consideration was being given to the most appropriate form of commemoration for those involved in the events in Jadotville and I am pleased to be in a position to report on the progress made since then.

I have decided that a plaque will be situated in Athlone to commemorate the events at Jadotville and the very significant contribution of A company and of the 35th battalion, as a whole, to the UN peace support mission in the Congo. To this end, discussions are ongoing at present in the Western Brigade regarding the siting of this plaque.

I have also decided that portraits of Lieutenant Colonel McNamee, 35th Battalion commander, and Commandant Quinlan, company commander A Company, will be commissioned and arrangements in this regard are under way. Once completed, it is intended that these portraits will hang in the Congo Room in the United Nations Training School in the Curragh.

For the men of Jadotville who felt their honor was tainted and their CO's memory left under a cloud, vindication had arrived. More importantly, the Jadotville chapter of Ireland's military and UN history does not have to remain closed to future generations.

The lessons that can be learned from the episode are many, and probably the most significant concerns the telling effect of good leadership in adversity. As John Gorman said: "Comdt. Quinlan saved our lives because we trusted him with them ... totally!"

But then again, there was another factor in being able to survive the siege at Jadotville. As Comdt. Quinlan noted in his after-action report, he "never once saw any man waver...Their steadfastness and coolness under heavy fire was extraordinary."

ACKNOWLEDGEMENTS

B ooks can only be possible through provision of information. That information must flow to the author through a conduit, and these conduits are more commonly known as people. It was through a conversation with a now retired soldier, Cpl. Tony McAnaney of the 4th Field Artillery Regiment (FAR), whose father, John, served at Jadotville, that I was introduced to this story.

My service in the Army, both regular and reserve, between the late eighties and 1999 introduced me to a variety of characters, particularly in the 9th and 4th FAR, who inculcated in me a love of our more recent military history. The foundations laid then were also the foundations for this book.

However, this book was only made possible by the cooperation of a number of the veterans of A Company, 35th Battalion—the men of Jadotville.

In particular, I would like to express my thanks to John Gorman from Horseleap in Moate, Co. Westmeath, who was so generous with his time and his opinions of the Jadotville period. I am grateful for access to his private papers and photos which have assisted me in writing this book.

Although only a young soldier at the time, John never forgot his comrades and has been to the fore in lobbying the government for some form of recognition for his comrades and their families. John was also a very helpful link man who put me in touch with other veterans whose information played a pivotal role in this book.

These men included retired BQMS Pat Neville. Though well into his eighties, he was able to regale me with stories about life in the Army during its infancy in the 1930s. He painted a picture of a tough existence that laid the foundation for the Army's successes in the Congo.

The personal diary of Walter Hegarty DSM, the once-youthful platoon sergeant of No. 2 Platoon, paints a vivid picture of what the young soldiers of A Company faced at Jadotville. In addition, he painstakingly copied documents, letters, and diaries as well as pictures for inclusion in this book.

Walter was ever patient in explaining the lead up to Jadotville from an infantry soldier's viewpoint. Having met him, it came as no surprise to learn that he was later to be decorated with the Distinguished Service Medal for displaying "outstanding leadership, resourcefulness, and courage" under enemy fire at a later date after Jadotville.

Retired Capt. Noel Carey, although typical of many veterans who do not like to talk directly about their role in action, was persuaded to give me unprecedented access to his personal papers of the time.

I am deeply appreciative of this, for his commentary is unguarded, candid, and searingly honest about his experience. His diary was also of considerable help in establishing a narrative theme that ordered many of the other anecdotal accounts I received from veterans.

Other veterans who helped by giving me their reminiscences

include the men of the Irish United Nations Veterans Association (IUNVA), Post 20, in Mullingar.

Men such as Sgt. William (Bob) Allen (Ret.) (also later to be decorated with the DSM), Sgt. Bill Ready (Ret.) and Gnr. Tom Cunningham (Ret.), spoke at length to me over the years about their experience. I also owe my thanks to former BQMS Eddie Robinson, for his assistance with information and photographs at other times when I was researching the Jadotville story.

Even though he wore no uniform, retired *Irish Times* journalist Cathal O'Shannon can rightly be described as a veteran of the Congo. I thank him now for taking the time to talk to me as we approached Christmas even though he was recovering from jet lag and recent illness. Although not present at Jadotville, he reported extensively from the Congo and his anecdotes from this time helped put a number of things in context.

Of course, there are other people who probably aren't even aware of the role they played in bringing this project to fruition, and of course some who undoubtedly are more than aware.

My parents, Maura and Anthony Power, showed a decidedly greater enthusiasm for the project than I was feeling myself at times. Their foresight in hunting me out of the comfort of the family home post-Christmas and making me go back to work in Dublin is appreciated, I think!

My former and last commanding officer from army days, Comdt. Eoghan Ó Neachtain (Ret.), is a man whose friendship, direction, and mentoring has had no small effect on my life. He surely gave me the best advice in completing this project as I tended towards wallowing in research for far too long: "Kill it, kill it now! Don't let it drag on."

Appropriate advice from a former artillery officer.

I would like to thank Commandants Victor Laing and Pat Brennan as well as the non-commissioned staff of Military Archives who were always willing to be of assistance with documentation.

I would also like to thank the following for their assistance: Ken Foxe, Cormac Bourke, Barry Owens, Aidan Crawley, and Ron Quinlan. Also Jean Harrington, John Mooney, and Alicia McAuley of Maverick House.

Thanks too to the others who helped but must stay anonymous by nature of their appointments.

Declan Power. Dublin, March 2005.

A COMPANY ROLL

"A" Company roll with attached personnel
(while at Jadotville and later in captivity as per Red Cross listing)

RANK AND NAME, APPOINTMENT, DOB

Officers and Senior NCOs—A Company, 35th Battalion
Comdt. Patrick Joseph Quinlan, Company Commander, 1.23.19
Comdt. Joseph Patrick Clune, Doctor, 3.22.27
Capt. Dermot Byrne, Second in Command, 12.4.23
Capt. William (Liam) Donnelly, Platoon Commander, 12.5.28
Capt. Thomas McGuinn, Platoon Commander, 3.15.18
Lt. William Noel Carey, Platoon Commander, 1.2.36
Lt. Joseph Anthony Oliver Leech, Platoon Commander, 5.29.33
Lt. Thomas Quinlan, Platoon Commander, 1.24.34
Lt. Kevin Paschal Knightly, Armored Car Det. Commander, 10.27.32

Fr. Thomas Fagan, Chaplain, 9.18.18
C/S John Prendergast, Company Sergeant, 2.2.15
CQMS Patrick Neville, Quartermaster Sergeant, 11.24.18

Attached Swedish Personnel
2/Lt. R. Larse Fromberg, Swedish Liaison Officer, 11.25.26
W/Officer Eric O. Thors, Helicopter Copilot, 8.21.36

Attached Norwegian Personnel
Lt. Bjarne Hovden, Helicopter Pilot, 2.17.22

Attached UN Civilian Personnel
Mr. Michael Nolan (Irish), UN Civil Affairs, 2.10.08
Officer and Interpreter

NCOs and Men, A Company, 35th Battalion
Corporal William Allen, 9.28.25
Private Gerald Battles, 8.5.42
Private Francis Leo Boland, 4.18.39
Private Joseph Daniel Bracken, 10.6.41
Private Robert Laurence Bradley, 8.30.38
Corporal Colm Brannigan, 1.5.40
Private Michael Gerrard Brennan, 10.17.39
Private John Broderick, 7.21.41
Private Michael Broderick, 5.21.43
Corporal Patrick Bourke, 2.26.39
Private James Byrne, 8.13.30
Private Patrick Conlon, 3.12.40
Private Desmond Connolly, 4.23.33
Private John Conway, 7.9.41
Private Charles John Cooley, 6.16.42
Sergeant Geoffrey Patrick Cuffe, 6.22.34

Gunner Thomas Cunningham, 3.14.39

Private Patrick Delaney, 5.18.42

Private Albert Arthur Dell, 2.20.25

Corporal James Dempsey, 10.1.34

Corporal John Oliver Devine, 7.9.38

Sergeant Henry Dixon, 9.30.24

Corporal John Donnelly, 3.10.39

Private Patrick Donnelly, 12.3.41

Private John Joseph Dowler, 6.10.41

Private Joseph Duff, 6.12.24

Private Patrick Duffy, 12.17.19

Private William George Duffy, 5.4.38

Private Maurice Doyle, 9.18.41

Private John Dreelin, 4.4.43

Private Patrick Dunleavy, 4.11.42

Private Anthony Dykes, 11.12.41

Private James William Feery, 7.11.40

Private Simon James Finlass, 10.9.37

Private Dominic Flaherty, 2.6.22

Private John Flynn, 9.25.40

Private John William Flynn, 4.8.38

Private Thomas Flynn, 11.2.42

Corporal John Foley, 3.15.40

Corporal John James Foster, 9.14.30

Private Michael Joseph Galvin, 1.6.42

Private Patrick Gildea, 9.17.17

Sergeant Francis Gilsenan, 12.18.21

Private John Gorman, 4.20.41

Private Edward James Gormley, 6.16.40

Private Noel Francis Graham, 12.29.41

Private Michael Greene, 7.2.41

Gunner Thomas Patrick Gunne, 3.10.38

Private William Francis Hannigan, 8.10.37

Private Dominic Harkin, 2.2.38

Private James Harper, 9.29.40

Gunner William Heffernan, 12.20.24

Private Daniel Hegarty, 5.5.42

Private Henry Hegarty, 1.7.42

Private Joseph Gerard Hegarty, 11.5.39

Sergeant Walter Thomas Hegarty, 6.21.32

Private Gerald Hennelly, 2.13.42

Private Patrick Francis Hogan, 10.1.40

Private Thomas Michael, 10.14.42

Private William Henry Hughes, 6.3.40

Sergeant Patrick Joseph Joyce, 3.21.16

Private James Kavanagh, 9.23.38

Private William Francis Keene, 2.13.40

Sergeant Thomas Kelly, 2.9.24

Corporal Thomas Kerr, 11.6.35

Corporal Brendan Leffere, 6.12.38

Private Robert Patrick Larkin, 1.20.38

Private Thomas Michael Larkin, 3.21.41

Private Kieran Vincent Lynch, 1.4.35

Corporal Michael Lynch, 12.24.24

Private Edward Maher, 10.15.41

Private Francis Paul Malone, 9.6.42

Private Joseph Anthony Maloney, 11.3.40

Private Donal Michael Manley, 9.5.41

Private John Christopher Manning, 12.24.41

Private James Megley, 6.11.40

Private Daniel Molloy, 9.18.38

Sergeant John Gerard Monaghan, 4.12.34

Private Patrick Joseph Monaghan, 1.17.42

Private James Murray, 12.12.11

Private Myler (Lieutenant Carey's radio man—left off original
Red Cross POW listing)

Corporal John McAnaney, 11.3.21

Corporal James McArdle, 8.14.31

Sergeant Martin McCabe, 9.1.17

Private James McCourt, 12.3.36

Private Michael McCormack, 12.19.27

Private Michael James McDermott, 1.1.40

Corporal John McDonagh, 6.3.24

Private Thomas McDonagh, 9.29.42

Corporal Thomas Francis McDonnell, 1.9.34

Corporal John McEntee, 9.19.19

Private Matthew James McGrath, 1.2.41

Private Joseph McGuinness, 12.19.41

Sergeant Kevin Christopher McLoughlin, 12.29.21

Private Terence McMahon, 10.18.42

Private Francis McManus, 11.24.41

Corporal John Francis McManus, 12.12.32

Private Anthony McNerney, 10.9.27

Private John James Nicell, 6.11.41

Corporal John O'Brien, 2.20.24

Corporal Peter Joseph O'Callaghan, 6.13.34

Corporal Michael John O'Connor, 4.9.27

Private Michael Sean O'Farrell, 2.12.41

Private James Patrick O'Kane, 6.21.38

Private Joseph Alphonsus O'Kane, 10.5.36

Private Robert Orr, 11.12.42

Private Michael O'Sullivan, 4.26.40

Gunner John Francis Peppard, 11.4.28

Private Christopher Powell, 1.6.43

Private John Donald Purtill, 8.12.42

Private Martin Quinn, 8.21.43

Corporal Timothy Quinn, 12.28.42

Sergeant James Rea, 4.5.36

Private James Redmond, 7.22.42

Corporal Patrick Rhatigan, 3.17.41

Private Daniel Regan, 5.9.43

Private Joseph Relihan, 12.25.25

Private William Riggs, 6.1.32

Corporal Christopher John Roche, 12.20.28

Private Anthony Roper, 4.28.42

Gunner James Joseph Scally, 10.19.33

Gunner Michael Joseph Seery, 10.9.32

Private John Vincent Shanagher, 2.8.41

Corporal Michael Joseph Smith, 11.7.36

Private John Joseph Stanford, 9.27.40

Private Noel Stanley, 1.1.40

Private Timothy Sullivan, 10.22.41

Private Bernard Sweeney, 2.14.25

Private Phillip James Sweeney, 7.1.40

Private James Joseph Tahaney, 7.2.42

Sergeant George Francis Tiernan, 4.19.25

Corporal Sean Tiernan, 12.19.42

Private Michael John Tighe, 2.22.39

Private Charles Tomkins, 12.29.09

Private Patrick Joseph Williams, 5.2.34

Attached Armored Car Crews and Maintenance Personnel
Sergeant Colman Geary, 13.2.35

Corporal Thomas O'Connor, 13.5.41

Corporal James Lucey, 24.9.40

Trooper Patrick McCarton, 22.9.39

Trooper Michael Nolan, 18.7.43

Trooper John Shanahan, 19.7.22

Trooper Joseph O'Brien, 3.5.20
Private Michael Dunne, 25.2.39
Private William Ready, 24.4.41

SUMMARY OF IMPORTANT DATES

1961

May 30:   A Company assembles at Custume Barracks, Athlone.

June 16:   Company are activated and move to Curragh. Embark at Dublin Airport for the Congo.

June 25:   Arrive at Elisabethville.

July 13:   No. 2 Platoon with Lt. Quinlan in command go to Louvanium University in Léopoldville. On duty for assembly of Central Congo Government.

Aug. 1:   Move from Factory Camp to Sabena Villas.

Aug. 23:   Patrol to Dilolo, Capt. Byrne in command.

Aug. 27:   Operation to capture members of gendarmerie at Airport in Elisabethville in cooperation with B Company.

Aug. 30: Operation Rumpunch—capture of gendarmerie HQ in Elisabethville by A Company.

Sept. 3: A Company ordered to move to Jadotville. Move completed September 4.

Sept. 6: Patrol to Kolwezi, Lt. Leech and Lt. Knightly.

Sept. 9: Katangan gendarmes surround A Company position at Jadotville. Supplies refused by traders.

Sept. 13: Katangans launch sneak attack.

Sept. 16: Katangans ask for cease-fire.

Sept. 17: Cease-fire negotiations end with the surrender of A Company.

Sept. 23: Comdt. Cahalane, Lt. Ryan, and other Irish and Italian prisoners captured in Elisabethville brought to join A Company in captivity at Jadotville.

Oct. 11: Transferred to a new prison camp at Kolwezi.

Oct. 17: Prisoners brought to Camp Massart in Elisabethville for release but returned again to Kolwezi still as prisoners.

Oct. 25: All prisoners released at old airstrip in Elisabethville.

Nov. 28: Advance party of A Company leave for home. Capt. Donnelly, Lt. Carey, 58 NCOs, and men.

Dec. 5: Fighting breaks out again in Elisabethville. Lt. Quinlan with No. 2 platoon engaged in fighting at old airstrip.

Dec. 12: Destruction of Soco petrol station.

Dec. 23: Last Globemaster home to Dublin and then to Athlone.

GLOSSARY OF TERMS

RANK STRUCTURE OF THE IRISH ARMY

Private (Pte.): There are two grades, private two star and private three star. Most, if not all, privates in the Congo would have been three-star grade. This denotes that they were fully trained soldiers in both infantry and corps duties.

Gunner (Gnr.): This is the private three-star grade of the Artillery Corps. While many of the Corps served in an artillery capacity, some served as infantry soldiers, as can be seen in the A Company Roll.

Trooper (Tpr.): This is the private three-star grade of the Cavalry Corps. These men served as armored car crews.

Non-Commissioned Officers (NCOs): The career soldiers are trained to be the first line supervisors, instructors, and discipline enforcers of an army.

NCO RANKS REFERRED TO IN THIS BOOK:

Corporal (Cpl.); Sergeant (Sgt.): Both of these ranks are concerned with commanding a section of approximately eight or nine men, except in the case of the Platoon Sergeant. He is the senior NCO rank in a platoon, which normally constitutes three fighting sections. The Platoon Sergeant answers to the Platoon Commander, usually a Lieutenant or a Junior Captain.

Company Quartermaster Sergeant (CQMS); Company Sergeant (C/S): These are the two senior NCO ranks at company level. CQMS is the equivalent of a Color or Staff Sergeant in the British Army. He would equate with a Staff or Sergeant First Class in the US Army. The CQMS looks after the logistics and welfare needs of the men in his Company. The C/S is equivalent to a Company Sergeant Major or CSM in the British Army and a 1st Sergeant in the US Army. He is the senior Sergeant in the Company and acts as the principal link between the troops and the Company Commander, much like a Bo'sun in the Navy.

Battalion Quartermaster Sergeant (BQMS): As for CQMS, but at a higher level.

Battalion Sergeant Major (BSM): As for C/S, but at battalion level. Both BQMS and BSM are considered to be of equivalent status to the rank of Warrant Officer.

Commissioned Officer: The planners and senior executive management of an army.

THE FOLLOWING ARE THE COMMISSIONED OFFICER RANKS REFERRED TO IN THIS BOOK:

Second Lieutenant (2/Lt.); Lieutenant (Lt.): Both these ranks are principally Platoon Commanders. These are the most junior officers, usually in their early to midtwenties.

Captain (Capt.): The principal grade of junior officer at Company level. The captain grade would fill 2IC appointments in the Company and junior staff officer functions at battalion level. He is expected to be experienced with leading men at subunit level as well as carrying out junior-level staff and planning assignments.

Commandant (Comdt.): This rank is equivalent to rank of Major in most other military forces. It is the rank that commences an officer's step onto more senior leadership appointments in his career. The command of a Company represents a move towards more autonomous command. Usually a proven and experienced officer in his late thirties upwards. Also fulfils important planning appointments at staff level in Battalion HQ.

Lieutenant Colonel (Lt. Col.): Usually the grade at which a battalion is commanded. A lieutenant colonel would also fill staff appointments at Force or Army HQ regarding planning or operations.

Colonel (Col.): Senior officer grade before the General ranks start. Usually commands a defense establishment or school or acts in staff appointments at Headquarter level. In the Irish Defence Forces all the corps directorates, such as Artillery, Engineers, Communication, and Information Services (the old Signal Corps), are commanded by Colonels. Essential HQ Staff appointments such as the Directorates of Training and Intelligence are also commanded by Colonel rank.

Brigadier General (Brig. Gen.): First of the General officer ranks, and in most armies commands at Brigade level. In the Irish Defence Forces, the officer that commands one of the Brigade areas such as the Western, Eastern, Southern, formerly known as Commands. Equivalent in rank to a British Army Brigadier and the naval rank of Commodore, the senior rank of the Irish

Naval Service. Also the senior officer rank of the Air Corps and the Defence Force Training Centre at the Curragh Camp.

Major General (Major Gen.): Usually the rank at which a division is commanded. One of the senior executive ranks in the Irish Defence Forces. There are two Major Gens., one in the appointment of Deputy Chief of Staff (Operations), the old Adjutant-General role and Deputy Chief of Staff (Support), the old Quartermaster General role. Operations looks after the day to day missions and discipline of the Defence Forces at home and abroad. Support looks after all issues of military supply and logistics both at home and abroad.

Lieutenant General (Lt. Gen.): The chief executive rank of the Irish Defence Forces, otherwise known as the Chief of Staff. This rank reports directly to the Minister for Defence and is responsible for implementing the Minister's directions and Governmental policy regarding defense matters.

UNIT HIERARCHY OF THE IRISH TROOPS SERVING WITH ONUC IN 1961

"A" Company was a subunit of the 35th Irish Battalion serving with UN forces (ONUC) in the Congo. This unit structure is virtually unchanged today and parallels the structure of most western armies such as the US or UK forces.

Battalion (Bn. or Batt.): The largest Irish formation was a battalion, the 35th Battalion, consisting of four companies, "A," "B," "C," and "Headquarter" Company. With the exception of HQ Company, each company generally consisted of approximately 150 men (not including any attachments). It would normally be assigned a region in which to secure and patrol on the orders of the overall Force Commander.

The battalion is commanded by a Lieutenant Colonel. It is

he who would implement the Force Commander's orders and deal with all operational matters within his battalion area. The Battalion Commander would be assisted by a staff of officers at the rank of Commandant and Captain, as well as a number of NCOs such as the Sergeant Major, in implementing his orders, drawing up plans for attaining objectives, and overseeing logistics operations.

Company (Coy): The company is a semiautonomous formation of the battalion. Generally, a company would be dispatched to carry out a task such as securing an area of terrain, as "A" Company was assigned to do. On a peacekeeping operation, the companies of a battalion would have the region assigned divided up between them. The company is commanded by a commandant. He is assisted in running the company by two senior sergeants who look after logistics and discipline, and a senior captain who acts as 2IC.

Platoon (Pl.): In most western armies this is the smallest formation commanded by a commissioned officer, usually a Lieutenant. In the case of the weapons platoon, it may be a more experienced officer such as a Captain. The platoon rarely operates independently of the Company and the platoon commander is usually in direct contact with his Company Commander during all operations.

There are usually three rifle platoons and one weapons platoon. The Weapons Platoon is made up of extra weaponry such as sixty mm and eighty-one mm mortars, heavy machine guns which give the Company an ability to defend itself across greater ranges and distances.

The platoon comprises approximately thirty-two men including NCO ranks such as Corporal and Sergeant. These ranks assist the lieutenant in leading the platoon on operations. The lieutenant's principal assistant is the platoon sergeant, an

NCO qualified to take charge of the platoon. Sometimes this NCO is older and more experienced than the lieutenant. It is he who will generally supervise the men and see to their welfare, while the lieutenant makes out his plans based on orders received from his company commander.

Section: Known as the "squad" in the US Army, this was the smallest of formations in the Irish contingent operating in the Congo. In the Irish Army a section is commanded by a Corporal or a junior Sergeant. He is assisted by a junior corporal known as the section 2IC. The section is made up of approximately eight men. They are all rifle men except for the LMG gunner and his assistant. It is they who provide the covering fire for the section when putting in an attack.

WEAPONS

Browning Automatic Pistol (BAP): The Browning was the new pistol on issue to officers, senior NCOs and transport crews. It fired 9 mm ammunition and was much more accurate than the old issue Webley revolver. The BAP is still in use today by the Irish Defence Forces.

FN (Fabrique Nationale) rifle: The new automatic self-loading rifle (SLR) Irish troops were issued with while serving in the Congo. It fired 7.62 caliber ammunition similar to most NATO countries and replaced the old WWII vintage .303 Lee-Enfield.

Light Machine Gun (LMG): In this case it was generally the WWII vintage Bren gun which fired .303 caliber ammunition. It was later replaced by the General Purpose Machine Gun (GPMG) similar to the one used by the British Army. The LMG provides the main firepower for a section of troops.

Mortar: A type of infantry support weapon. It literally fires a bomb into the air to land on opposing forces. In the right hands it can be a devastating piece of firepower as it gives a force the ability to bring fire to bear on targets out of line of sight. They vary in caliber between 60 mm, 81 mm, and the 120 mm heavy mortar.

Submachine Gun (SMG): The weapon of this category used by Irish troops in the Congo was the Carl Gustaf SMG which fired 9 mm caliber ammunition. This caliber of ammunition was the same as used in a pistol which meant the SMG didn't have much of a range. It could be used effectively in close-quarter combat and was favored by officers, senior NCOs, and crews of armored and soft-skin vehicles.

OTHER TERMS

Adjutant (Adj.): The staff officer responsible for personnel and administrative matters at Battalion and Brigade level. Usually a Captain or Commandant.

Artillery (Arty.): Heavy weapons that need a crew to fire them, generally referred to as cannons by civilians. Used to support infantry in attack and defense.

Cavalry: Used to refer to horse-mounted troops, but now refers to troops armed with light armored vehicles.

Commanding Officer (CO): Generally refers to the senior officer commanding at a particular location such as a garrison or barracks.

Corps: The different specialties other than infantry in an army. For example, artillery, signals, engineers, etc.

Distinguished Service Medal (DSM): The second highest decoration for valor in the Irish Defence Forces.

Fórsa Cosanta Áitiúil (FCA): Translated from Irish this means Local Defence Force.

Garrison: A military detachment tasked with providing a static presence in a town or city.

Headquarters (HQ): Each formation from Company upwards will have a HQ element comprising the CO, his 2IC, his signalers, clerks, and other staff.

Infantry: Foot soldiers who do most of the up-close and personal fighting and dying.

Officer Commanding (OC): Generally refers to officers commanding formations of battalion size upwards.

Quartermaster (QM): The staff officer concerned with all logistic matters at either Battalion or Brigade level.

Regiment: A formation of troops that used to incorporate one or more battalions, that is, four hundred to five hundred men. In the Irish Defence Forces a regiment refers to an artillery unit of approximately two hundred men.

Second-in-Command (2IC or 2I/C): The 2IC is the universal military abbreviation for the officer or NCO filling this appointment. At Company level this would usually be a Captain; at Battalion level it would be a Commandant.

Warrant Officer (W/O): This is a rank equivalent to BSM or BQMS in the Irish Army.

LIST OF SOURCES

BOOKS

Cruise O'Brien, Conor. *To Katanga and Back*. London: Hutchison, 1962.

De Witte, Ludo. *The Assassination of Lumumba*. London: Verso, 2002.

Mockler, Anthony. *The New Mercenaries*. London: Sidgwick and Jackson Limited, 1985.

O'Farrell, Mick. *Tough At The Bottom*. Dublin: Arriba Publications, 1999.

Smith, Raymond. *Under The Blue Flag*. Dublin: Aherlow Press, 1980.

Smith, Raymond. *The Fighting Irish in the Congo*. Dublin: Lilmac (Little and McClean), 1962.

Rikhye, I. J. *UN Peacekeeping and the Congo Crisis*. London: Hurst, 1993.

United Nations. *The Peacekeeper's Handbook*. New York: International Peace Academy, 1978.

United Nations. *The Blue Helmets*. New York: UN Dept. of Public Information, 1990.

von Horn, Carl. *Soldiering for Peace*. London: Casell, 1966.

JOURNALS AND STUDIES

Bloomer, David R. *Violence in the Congo—A Perspective of United Nation's Peacekeeping*. Subject area: Foreign Policy 2, Marine Corps Command and Staff College, April 1984.

Carr, T., P. Carey, D. Dignam, F. Lawless and D. O'Neill, UN Operations in the Congo, 1960–1962. 5th Junior Command and Staff Course, Irish Defence Force Military College, the Curragh, 1995.

Dorn, Walter. "The Cloak and the Blue Beret—The Limits of Intelligence Gathering in UN Peacekeeping." *Pearson Papers, No. 4: Intelligence in Peacekeeping*. Clementsport,

Nova Scotia: The Lester B. Pearson Canadian International Peacekeeping Centre, 1999

Dorn, Walter, and David J. H. Bell, "Intelligence and Peacekeeping: The UN Operation in the Congo 1960–64." *International Peacekeeping, Vol. 2, No. 1* (Spring 1995).

Hays, Geoff, and Sean M. Maloney, "Canadian Peacekeeping and the Congo, 1960–1964." *Gaffen, Fred, Position Paper 4*, Ontario: Waterloo University, November 18, 2003.

O'Neill, J. T., "The Irish Company at Jadotville, Congo, 1961: Soldiers or Symbols?" *International Peacekeeping, Vol. 9*, Winter 2002, No 4. London: Crown House, 2002.

IRISH DEFENCE FORCE MILITARY ARCHIVES

History of the 35th battalion in the Congo 1961.

The Battle of Jadotville—Appendix B, History 35th Bn.

Confidential after-action report of Comdt. Patrick Quinlan to Gen. Sean McKeown, October 30, 1961 (concerns the events surrounding Jadotville prior to Gen. McKeown's return to Ireland to brief the Government on events involving Irish troops).

After-action reports of A Company platoon commanders, October 1961.

A and B company commanders' reports on Elisabethville Airport action, August 26/27, 1961. Appendix M, History 35th Bn.

Operation Morthor—Headquarters, Sector B E'ville, Appendix A, History 35th Bn. (Includes signal traffic).

Operation Morthor Actions—C Company, September 27, 1961. Appendix D, History 35th Bn.

Confidential Letter of Appreciation of Service of 35th Irish Battalion from Brigadier Raja, Commanding Officer, Katanga Command ONUC to Force Commander in Léopoldville, no. 1004/7/GS, December 2, 1961 (includes specific mention of Comdt. Quinlan and A Company at Jadotville).

Orduithe Gnáthaimh Ginearalta (General Routine Orders)—OGG 10, 1967 Department of Defence (document concerning awards of DSMs for actions during Congo operation).

Report of Charles Kearney to Irish Battalion HQ following Jadotville siege.

NEWSPAPER ARTICLES

Power, Declan. "UN Vets Remember Jadotville." *Sunday World*, April 20, 2001

Power, Declan. "UN Vets Medal Shame." *Sunday Mirror,* May 5, 2002

Power, Declan. "Humbled in the Jungle." *Ireland on Sunday,* May 9, 2004.

Smith, R. "Jadotville Post Over-Run." *Irish Independent*, September 18, 1961.

Younghusband, Peter. "The Tigers of Jadotville." *Daily Mail*, September 23, 1961

WEBSITES USED FOR BACKGROUND RESEARCH

[Author unknown], *Livre blanc du gouvernement katangais sur les évenements de septembre et decembre 1961*, http://users.skynet.be/christhel/katanga/livreblanc/

Chopra, Pushpindar Singh, William Green, and Gordon Swanborough, eds. "Canberras in the Congo." *The Indian Air Force and Its Aircraft, IAF Golden Jubilee,* 1932–1982, London: Dulcimus Books, 1982, reproduced at www.bharat-rakshak.com/IAF.History/Congo

Department of National Defence Canadian Forces, www.forces.gc.ca

Sherry, Gerard E. "Editor Triggers US Atrocity into Congo Atrocities." *The Georgia Bulletin*, (Print Issue: 31 January 1963), http://www.georgiabulletin.org/

INDEX

Y